D1262848

GRIZZLY BEARS AND RAZOR CLAMS

Walking America's Pacific Northwest Trail

Chris Townsend

SANDSTONEPRESS
HIGHLAND | SCOTLAND

First published in Great Britain in 2012
Sandstone Press Ltd
PO Box 5725
One High Street
Dingwall
IV15 9WJ
Scotland

www.sandstonepress.com

All rights reserved.

No part of this publication may be reproduced, stored or transmitted in any form without the express, written permission of the publisher.

Editor: Robert Davidson

Maps created by David Langworth, Melrose

© Chris Townsend 2012

© All photographs Chris Townsend 2012

The moral right of Chris Townsend to be recognised as the author of this work has been asserted in accordance with the Copyright, Design and Patents Act, 1988.

The publisher acknowledges support from Creative Scotland towards publication of this volume.

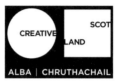

ISBN: 978-1-908737-04-5

Book design by Heather Macpherson @ Raspberryhmac, Edinburgh

Printed and bound in the EU

Back cover image:
On Cathedral Pass, Pasyaten Wilderness, Cascade Mountains

R0427998480

ACKNOWLEDGEMENTS

Although the walk was a solo effort many people actually helped to make it and this book possible. Thanks are due to all of them.

Firstly, as always, my partner Denise Thorn for understanding my need to disappear off on long walks and for encouraging and supporting me in doing so.

Ron Strickland, of course, for creating the trail in the first place and also for sending me the guidebook and encouraging me to hike the trail.

My cousin, Kristina Gravette, for providing me with a base close to the trail and driving me to the start and from the finish. Her help made the logistics of the walk much easier. It was a pleasure to hike with her at the start and finish of the walk.

Jon Knechtel and the Pacific Northwest Trail Association for their work on the trail. All those hikers who posted useful information on the PNTA Message Board, especially 'mule' (Sam Haraldson).

Li Brannfors for supplying his excellent maps without which route finding would have been much harder.

The local people along the way who went out of their way to help a trail-stained hiker – Jessica and the staff of the Feist Creek restaurant; Mike of North Country Transportation; the owner of the Washington Hotel, Metaline Falls; the Mattesons in Northport; the driver who gave me a lift into Sedro Woolley; the North Cascades and Olympic National Park rangers who were helpful and understanding regarding permits; and the various other rangers and others in motels, stores and cafes who gave advice.

GoLIte for tent, pack, sleeping bag and windshirt and for responding so quickly (thanks Coup!) when I had a problem with my pack.

ViewRanger for topo maps of the whole trail plus GPS software for my smartphone.

Trail Designs for a Caldera Cone Inferno stove unit that fitted my Evernew pot.

Inov8 for two pairs of Terroc shoes.

Burton McCall, the UK distributors of Pacific Outdoor Equipment, for the Ether air bed.

Pacerpoles for their carbon fibre trekking poles.

Emily Rodway, editor of TGO, for running my updates on the walk in the magazine.

Robert Davidson of Sandstone Press for his enthusiasm and support and Heather Macpherson for the design.

Finally, all those working to conserve and restore the magnificent wild lands of the Pacific Northwest.

To Denise

THE PACIFIC NORTHWEST TRAIL

CHIEF MOUNTAIN TO CAPE ALAVA

July 20 – October 2

1200 miles/1931km

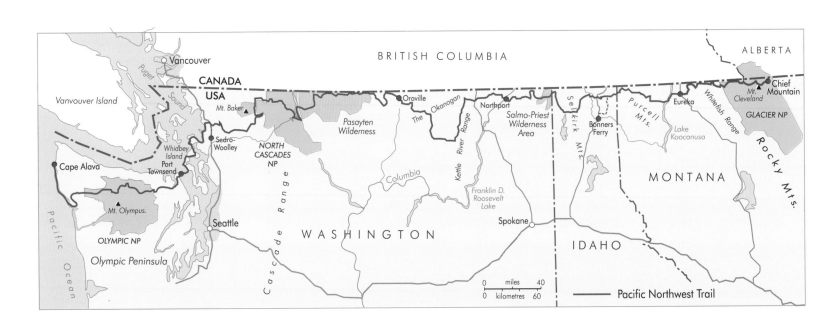

CONTENTS

INTRODUCTION

INSPIRATION & ORGANISATION

The Northwest USA is a land of mountains and forest, a wild land where bears and wolves roam. Through this magnificent country a route threads its way from the Rocky Mountains to the Pacific Ocean, passing through three national parks and seven national forests along the way. This is the Pacific Northwest Trail, a 1200 mile/1900 kilometre mix of signed footpaths, abandoned old trails, dirt roads, highways, animal tracks and cross-country hikes. Eventually a complete signposted trail may exist but it's a long way from that condition at present and hiking the PNT today is an adventure requiring route-finding skills and the ability to deal with difficult terrain. There is a guidebook but this is long out of date and despite having a route description is not detailed enough to make the route always easy to follow. It was more useful for advice, suggestions and a general overview. The guidebook author and PNT founder Ron Strickland says conditions range from perfectly built and groomed paths to 'hellish jungles' and warns that

'you are going to have to work to enjoy the Pacific Northwest Trail', which is just the sort of challenge that appeals to me.

Ron first came up with the idea for the PNT, which is one of the newer long distance trails in the USA, back in 1970 after which he spent many years working on building support for the trail. Since his initial exploration of possible routes the PNT has developed into today's network with new sections of trail being constructed every year under the auspices of the Pacific Northwest Trail Association. In 2009 the PNT became an official National Scenic Trail, which means it has U.S. government approval and backing.

Creating a long distance trail like the Pacific Northwest requires a phenomenal amount of work, energy and commitment. Routes have to be explored, trails constructed, signs erected, rivers bridged, information provided and amenities checked (natural campsites, water sources, viewpoints). The volunteers of the Pacific

Northwest Trail Association, founded in 1977, have spent thousands of hours on this work. Without them there would be no trail so every backpacker and hiker who loves long walks in wild country owes them gratitude. Providing a trail for walkers is only a starting point however. The real value of long distance trails is in the protection they give to the landscape through which they pass. As Ron Strickland says at the end of his PNT guidebook 'saving it for others is the ultimate challenge'.

Ron Strickland's idea all those years ago was for a trail running from the Continental Divide, the watershed of the USA, in the Rocky Mountains to the Pacific Ocean. As such the PNT begins in Glacier National Park in Montana, just south of the Canadian border. The Continental Divide Trail, which I had hiked 25 years earlier all the way from Canada to Mexico, begins at the same place and I began my walk along the length of the Canadian Rockies here too. Having already walked south and

View from the Stoney Indian Pass Trail over Atsina Lake to Glenns Lake and Cosley Lake, Glacier National Park

Ron Strickland (photo Ron Strickland)

north from this point the idea of beginning a third long walk and heading west from the same place was really appealing. Also, much further along in the Cascade Mountains the PNT crosses the Pacific

Crest Trail, which I'd hiked from Mexico to Canada, just south of its terminus at the Canadian border so I would be able to make a link with this walk as well.

I'd been thinking about hiking the Pacific Northwest Trail for many years, encouraged by Ron who'd sent me a copy of his guidebook. I liked the idea of an undeveloped route, much of it in remote and little-frequented wild places that I'd never visited before, and I loved the idea of again spending weeks in the mountains and forests, travelling on foot through the natural world. Other projects and schemes kept pushing the PNT to 'sometime in the future' but finally it was time to stop thinking and start walking and get rid of the nagging itch that I really should go and find out what it was like.

My plan was to start in July, when the previous winter's snow should have mostly gone and summer in the high mountains would be under way. Having begun the Continental Divide Trail in late May and struggled through deep unstable snow in Glacier National Park I knew that an early start was inadvisable. The weather was stormy too, with the mountains often shrouded in cloud, and my main memories of that first section of the CDT are of difficult and dangerous terrain and arduous

hiking. I hoped that by starting later I would be able to fully appreciate the glorious landscape of Glacier National Park. The weather in the Cascades on the Pacific Crest Trail had also been stormy and I had finished that trail with several days of constant rain, wet snow and low clouds, as the first wet autumn weather swept in. Again I hoped that this time I would be able to see the mountains as I would be there earlier when the weather should be more settled. This timescale is an advantage of a trail that is 1200 miles/1900 kilometres long rather than 2700 miles/4350 kilometres like the PCT or 3100 miles/5000 kilometres like the CDT. It's possible to hike it in a summer season without having to do very high mileages every day and there's no need to carry equipment for snow and ice. I wanted the time to immerse myself in the land and not constantly feel I had to push on to reach the finish before winter set in. The walk was about being there not simply blazing through.

Between the Rockies and the North Cascades the PNT runs through the Purcell and Selkirk Mountains, the Kettle River Range and the more arid sagebrush country of the Okanogan in the states of Montana, Idaho and Washington. All these regions would be new and exciting for me

and I was looking forward to exploring them. Much of the Rockies and the North Cascades would be new too, once I was away from the CDT and PCT. From the Cascades the trail descends to sea level at Samish Bay to the east of Vancouver Island. This isn't the end of the walk however as it follows the coast round to the Olympic Peninsula and then crosses the Olympic Mountains to the shores of the Pacific Ocean and Cape Alava, the westernmost point in the 48 contiguous states. With its rainforests and wild coast I was also relishing a first visit to the Olympic Peninsula. As I skimmed through the guidebook excitement was building.

As well as dealing with complex route finding and difficult rough terrain hiking the PNT also involves much ascent, with altitudes ranging from sea level to nearly 8000 feet/2400 metres. The terrain is mostly forest and mountain, with some coastal and more open drier sagebrush landscapes. The intention of the trail planners is that the PNT should stay in the mountains – 'as much as possible, the PNT keeps to the high country and its far horizons' (Ron Strickland). Temperatures can range from below freezing in the mountains to over 35°C in the Okanogan country so I needed to be able to deal with these

Ron Strickland prospecting the Pacific Northwest Trail in the Pasayten Wilderness in 1970 (photo Ron Strickland)

extremes. Rain was likely, especially in the Olympic Mountains, which records the highest rainfall in the continental USA ,and snow was possible in the highest areas of the Rockies and North Cascades while in the Okanogan and on the east side of the Olympics hot dry weather was just about certain.

Planning a long distance walk is, I find, a rather stop-go process. There is the initial burst of enthusiasm and excitement, which has me compiling gear lists, ordering maps and working out itineraries. Then there is a period of quiet and a return to normal activities, leaving the walk to lurk at the back of my mind. Occasionally something

relevant will catch my attention and I'll make some notes and do a little more planning. Over the months this can add up to a fair amount of work. Even so, there comes a point when I suddenly realise that actual decisions have to be made and everything from travel arrangements to gear to resupplies confirmed. This always seems to occur when the start of the walk is speeding towards me alarmingly fast so I have to plunge back into the task.

Some people like to know the route and plan their food in great detail. I do neither of these. I like an element of surprise. In fact I like as much surprise as possible. I don't want to know much about the landscape or the wildlife or even the trails. It's one reason I like routes like the Pacific Northwest Trail that are unfinished and offer a degree of challenge. I glanced at the guidebook and read the information on supply points but no more. I'd read the details as I went along – and vary the route if there was one I thought more interesting. Indeed, I knew that the guidebook, last revised some ten years earlier, was out-of-date with route changes and updates. At the last minute, when I was already in the States, long distance hiker Li Brannfors, whom I'd met in the High Sierra many years ago, offered to send me print-outs of maps with the PNT route he'd hiked the previous year marked on them plus sections of a revised guidebook that had not yet been published. These were mailed to my supply points so I only saw them as I arrived in each area and I didn't know in advance how Li's route would vary from that in the original guidebook.

I planned on resupplying along the way as far as possible, only sending food to the one place with no grocery store. This makes food supplies more interesting as small stores in little towns can have limited choice, especially in foods suitable for backpacking. I also planned on using a 'bounce' box – a large cardboard box containing maps for

![Backcountry Permit for Glacier National Park]

Glacier National Park
Montana

Backcountry Permit

PERMIT #2885   DATE: 07/19/2010 ISSUED: AP   #CAMPERS: 1   #SITES: 1   #STOCK: 0   #BOATS: 0

GLACIER
NATIONAL PARK
NON-TRANSFERABLE

DATE	ITINERARY	FIRES	LENGTH	ELEV UP	ELEV DN
ENTER	CHIEF MOUNTAIN TRAILHEAD	NO	13.30	315	744
07/20	MOKOWANIS JUNCTION CAMPGROUND	YES	13.20	2410	3125
07/21	GOAT HAUNT SHELTERS CAMPGROUND	YES	15.10	2050	2220
07/22	BOWMAN LAKE, HD CAMPGROUND		7.10	0	0
EXIT	BOWMAN LAKE FOOT (Akak,Bow,Qu) TRAILHEAD		48.70	4775	6089

11:05AM   Jul 19/10
00-0006 001   A9BC
#12876

3 x $5.00
$5 BC Permit $15.00

NAME: TOWNSEND, CHRIS   LICENSE1: NOCAR
ADDR: AUCHNARROW   CITY/ST/ZIP: GRANTOWN-ON-SPEY, UK PH263PL

CASH $15.00

Keep Your Receipt
VALID THRU
Jul 25/10

ADVISORIES: Hypothermia; Giardia; Bear/Lion; 25' rope to hang food; Early start recommended.
Solo not recomm; Snow hazard.

HANDOUTS:

- PLEASE NOTIFY NPS AT 888-7800 IF YOU CANCEL PART OF YOUR ITINERARY -

Backcountry Permit for Glacier National Park

the next section, town clothes, battery chargers, surplus food and other items – that would be sent ahead from post office to post office.

For this walk I was very lucky in having a cousin, Kristina Gravette, in Issaquah near Seattle, not far from the western part of the route, who was prepared to act as my 'base camp', somewhere I could stay while sorting out the last details before starting the walk and where I could send no longer needed items such as used maps and contact if there were any problems. In fact Kris and her daughter Leanne decided that a week in Glacier National Park sounded a good idea so they'd drive me to the start, which saved a train and bus journey. As we sped through the rolling plains south of the mountains I'd be walking in I mused on the huge difference between foot and car travel.

It would take me over two months to walk back from the Rockies to near Seattle. It took just over a day to travel there, and that included a delay after Kris's van broke down and had to be towed to a town and another van hired. A night was spent in a campground south of the town of Kalispell, which felt like a practice camp before the real thing. In Kalispell I mailed two boxes. One contained ten days food and went to Ross Lake Resort, which lay in the

Not wilderness – Logan Pass. Glacier National Park

middle of a three-week section without anywhere to buy supplies. I wouldn't see that box again for seven weeks. The other box was my 'bounce' box, which went to the little town of Eureka, much to the postmistress's amusement – 'that's just up the road'. Maybe so, but it was the wrong direction for our journey and it would take me nine days to

walk there.

Finally reaching Glacier National Park we stopped in West Glacier, where I visited the National Park Office to collect the obligatory permit for overnight hiking, which cost $15. Before I could be issued with a permit I had to watch a video on backcountry safety, which I felt could do

with updating, and then be given the same advice on safety in bear country by the very friendly ranger. The advice was repeated on the permit, in leaflets and on a plastic bag provided for carrying out litter. There are both grizzly and black bears in Glacier and the park really does want visitors to know how to co-exist safely with them. Attacks are very rare but can be fatal when they occur – for the bear, which is usually shot, as well as people – so I guess the seemingly excessive advice is necessary.

My permit, which had to be displayed on my pack when hiking and on my tent when camping (it did come in a plastic bag), was densely packed with rules, regulations and advice. It contained my itinerary, agreed with the ranger (I had to go slightly farther on my first day as the backcountry campsite I had hoped to use was full – there are limited pitches at each site), with the names of the trails I would use and the campsites where I would stay. The details of my trip were exemplary with the length, ascent and descent for each day all listed. In total my four days in the park would involve 48.7 miles in distance, 4775 feet of ascent and 6089 feet of descent. After that I was on my own. The permit had advisories – 'Hypothermia; Giardia; Bear/Lion; 25' rope to hang food; Early start

At the start in Glacier National Park in the Rocky Mountains

recommended. Solo not recomm; Snow hazard'. I ignored the solo not recommended and hoped the snow hazard would be minimal. I reckoned I should be able to avoid hypothermia and giardia

and I would hang my food. I might even get some early starts.

Escaping from the park office we left West Glacier on the spectacular Going to the Sun road, which traverses the park via 6,646 foot/2,026 metre Logan Pass. The road, opened in 1933, is an amazing feat of engineering, winding round steep mountainsides in a series of great curves. The views are tremendous but have the quality of a video or postcard, being 'out there' while the spectator is 'in here'. There is no sense of involvement or immersion in the landscape. We stopped at Logan Pass, which I had crossed on foot on the Continental Divide Trail, and wandered amongst snow patches and spring flowers that gave just a touch of the feeling of being in the wilds. In the Visitor Centre I bought an interesting looking book – *The Abstract Wild* by Jack Turner – which I would read during the first week of the walk. As this passionate, angry and eloquent book is in part about letting the wild be wild and about the ersatz nature of the experience in managed wilderness like that of a national park it was ironic to find it in a park book store. In the core essay in the book Turner writes that 'in every manner conceivable national parks separate us from the freedom that is the promise of the wild'. In the first week of the

walk I was to experience exactly what Turner was writing about.

Dropping down from Logan Pass we found all the park campgrounds full and ended up outside the park on the almost empty Chewing Blackbones site on the edge of St Mary's Lake on the Blackfeet Indian Reservation. Just up the road was the excellent Two Sisters restaurant where we celebrated my walk, which would begin the next day. Back in camp a tremendous thunderstorm ensued with torrential rain and much lightning. Perhaps that's why my permit recommended early starts. Morning came with thick mist and then hazy sun with the tents laid out on the campground road to dry – it really was quiet. A café in Babbs provided a last meal of non-dried food and a store provided two cotton bandannas to replace the one I had already managed to lose. Now there was nothing to do but start.

A bank of wild flowers, foothills of the Cascade Mountains

CHAPTER 1

WILDERNESS TAMED, WILDERNESS WILD

THE ROCKY MOUNTAINS, CHIEF MOUNTAIN TO EUREKA

July 20–28

128 miles/206km

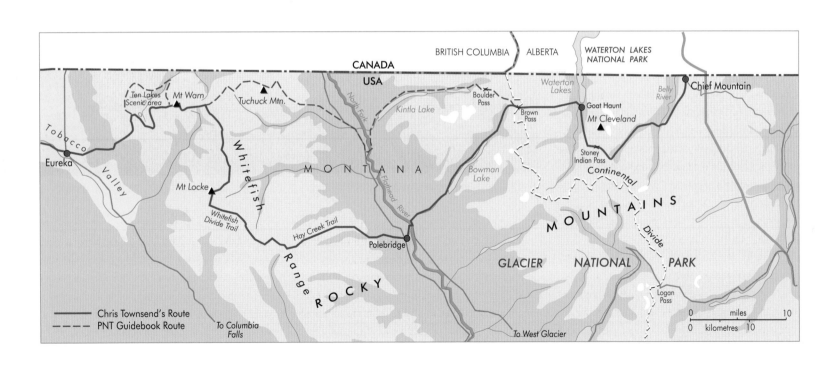

CANADA
USA

BRITISH COLUMBIA · ALBERTA · WATERTON LAKES NATIONAL PARK

Ten Lakes Scenic area · Mt Warn · Tuchuck Mtn. · North Fork · Boulder Pass · Waterton Lakes · Belly River · Chief Mountain

Kintla Lake · Brown Pass · Goat Haunt · Mt Cleveland

Tobacco Valley · Whitefish · MONTANA · Bowman Lake · Stoney Indian Pass · Continental

Eureka · Mt Locke · Flathead River · Divide

Whitefish Divide Trail · Hay Creek Trail · MOUNTAINS

Range · Polebridge · GLACIER NATIONAL PARK

ROCKY

To Columbia Falls · To West Glacier · Logan Pass

——— Chris Townsend's Route
- - - PNT Guidebook Route

0   miles   10
0   kilometres   10

Standing amongst the trees at the start of the Belly River Trail I looked down the narrow, winding path as it disappeared into the forest. This was it, the start of my summer in the wilds. Situated just south of the Canadian border at Chief Mountain the trailhead was pleasant but offered no hint of the tremendous landscape to come. It's not the most dramatic place for a long distance trail to start and indeed is a pragmatic choice rather than a desired one. The route used to start in Canada at the Waterton Lakes townsite and take the trail alongside Upper Waterton Lake into the USA. That's how I'd begun the Continental Divide Trail. By the time I came to hike the PNT international politics and border security had intervened. Entering the USA via a trail was no longer allowed if you weren't an American or Canadian and both the CDT and PNT shifted east to Chief Mountain and a trailhead as close to Canada as you could get without entering the country. This is a far cry from Ron Strickland's ideal route, which begins in Canada and takes a high mountain route into the USA.

Border politics aside – though they were to reappear several times during the walk – I was just happy to finally start hiking. There was no mention of the PNT on the signs at the trailhead, nor would I see a reference to it for many weeks. Taking my

The Belly River, Glacier National Park

first steps towards the Pacific I set off through the trees as the trail dropped down to the Belly River with occasional views of steep bare mountains that justified the name 'Rocky'. Kris and Leanne came as far as the river then headed back to Chief Mountain. I didn't expect to see them again for around three months. The trail was lined with masses of white flowered thimbleberries – a name I thought sounded like a fairy out of *A Midsummer Night's Dream*. Many other hikers were on the trail, most with huge packs that dwarfed mine, and there were many tents in the series of campgrounds I passed. A ranger stopped me and checked my permit, warning me that he'd seen a grizzly bear in the meadows by

First camp of the walk at Mokowanis Junction Campground, Glacier National Park

tent pitches, a 'food preparation area', a high bar for hanging food out of reach of bears and even a sketch map. Signs indicated each area and gave instructions – food was to be immediately hung and must never be taken to tent pitches. I duly obeyed – remembering the grizzly the ranger had seen – and hung my food bag before setting up camp. Then, feeling it was time for dinner, I realised I'd left the fuel for my stove in Kris's van. Luckily I'd brought a stove unit that could be used with wood as well as alcohol fuel, thinking it might be nice to have a mini-campfire occasionally and also so I didn't have to carry much fuel. I was going to be using it sooner than expected. A handful of twigs was soon gathered and lit and my first meal of the walk was cooking. I sat back and relaxed. Through the big spruce trees I could see the stark rock block of Pyramid Peak reaching into the sky. A movement distracted me from the mountain. A mule deer buck, its antlers in velvet, was wandering past just twenty feet away. Only a few mosquitoes broke the perfect feeling.

The Rocky Mountains in Glacier National Park have a distinctive layer-cake appearance. This is due to the many strata of sedimentary rocks of which they are built. These rocks were originally laid down in shallow seas some 1.6 billion to 800

Mokowanis Junction Campground, where I was to stay that night. He also guessed I was hiking the PNT from my lightweight pack and told me that he'd met another PNT hiker, Nimblewill Nomad, the day before. I was to hear of Nimblewill several times during my walk but never actually met him as he always stayed ahead of me.

I was surprised to find my campground empty. I guessed this was because it was in the woods while the ones I'd passed were close to lakeshores. I didn't mind. In fact I was happy to spend my first night on the trail alone and able to enjoy the peaceful evening with just bird song for accompaniment. The campground was highly organised with cleared

Paiota Falls, Atsina Falls and Cathedral Peak from the Stoney Indian Pass Trail, Glacier National Park

Trail sign and bear warning, Glacier National Park

a piece of paper by pushing the edges together. Despite the unimaginable figures for their age the Rockies are a young mountain range in geological terms. The Appalachian Mountains in the Eastern USA and my home mountains in the Scottish Highlands are both far older, dating from around 450 million years ago (and both are remnants of the same huge Caledonian Mountain range). New mountain ranges are high and steep with sharp pointed peaks, old mountain ranges are generally lower and more rounded. The final sculpting of the Rockies was done by the glaciers of the ice ages, which ended a mere 10,000 years ago. The slow moving powerful ice scoured out deep cirques and u-shaped valleys and shaved back the mountains to knife edge ridges and soaring peaks with huge rock faces. Rain, snow and ice still erode the mountains, slowly wearing them away. They are a mobile landscape, changing all the time. Looking out from my camp I could see the evidence for the geology on Cathedral and Pyramid Peaks, both showing the distinctive horizontal coloured bands of sedimentary rock and the narrow arêtes and sheer cliffs carved by the ice.

Oddly though, given the name, there are not many glaciers left in Glacier National Park and those remaining are shrinking as the climate warms. When the park was established in 1910 there were over 150 glaciers. There are only around a quarter of that number now. I was to see far more and much bigger glaciers in the Cascade Mountains much later in the walk. Glacier is a good place to see the effects of glaciers on the landscape but not glaciers themselves. What Glacier does have is rock mountains in every shape and form – spires, towers, ridges and more – with over 100 summits above 8,000 feet/2400 metres high. The highest, Mount Cleveland, reaches 10,479 feet/3194 metres.

Controlled and organised though Glacier National Park may be for human visitors it is still a wild place and one rich in wildlife. Doug Peacock, a man who has never bothered with rules and regulations, writes in his excellent book *Grizzly Years* 'that part of Montana around Glacier National Park is the last place left in the contiguous states where all the Rocky Mountain megafauna that was here when the white man showed up on the east coast can still be found: the wolf, the wolverine, the woodland caribou, and the grizzly'. Of these it's the grizzly that symbolises wilderness. Doug Peacock is a figure who haunts the imagination of anyone concerned about the conservation of the great wilderness areas of the American West. He came to fame as the model for

million years ago and then uplifted between 170 and 60 million years ago when tectonic plates collided along the western edge of North America and squeezed rock masses together, like crumpling

George Washington Hayduke in Edward Abbey's influential comic novel *The Monkey Wrench Gang*. Hayduke, whilst entertaining, is a fairly simple and crude character – though Jack Turner's description of him as 'stunted and pathetic' in *The Abstract Wild*, which I was reading in camp, is somewhat harsh. But the Doug Peacock revealed in Peacock's own books is far more complex, interesting and sympathetic. Returning from the Vietnam War, where he served as a medic, Peacock sought healing and refuge amongst the grizzlies in the wilderness. *Grizzly Years* is his story and tells how nature restored him. It's also a great defence of the bears and their land. Turner argues that Peacock is important, partly because of his love for grizzlies but also because he has begun 'a modern lore of grizzly bears', which Turner says is essential if we are not to lose the grizzly. This, I think, matters. We do need stories that give the bears a place, we do need an understanding that the value of wild places is diminished if big predators like the grizzly are absent and we do need to accept that the bears are out there, where they have every right to be and where they should remain.

Reading Jack Turner on Peacock as the day faded away I pondered one passage. After describing how Peacock often spent long periods of time alone in the wilderness, Turner writes 'this is extremely rare in the culture of modernity. I am certain that less than one percent of our population has ever spent a day in truly wild country, and the number who have done so alone is infinitesimal'. Maybe this is so. I don't know. I do know that after I have given a talk on one of my long walks one question often recurs – 'how do you cope with being alone?' Being alone is perceived as difficult or a problem. I have never found it so. I don't have to cope because there is nothing to cope with. I have spent much time alone in wild country, the longest single stretch without seeing another person being ten days in a remote area of the Yukon Territory.

View from Stoney Indian Pass, Glacier National Park

13

I do my long walks alone and whilst I may travel with others for short periods of time (for just three half days on this walk, including the first morning and the last afternoon) mostly I stay by myself. I am there to experience the natural world in all its aspects and I find this easiest to do by myself. That world is so rich and diverse that it occupies me fully. I am unaware of the absence of others.

Dawn came with mule deer in camp rather than grizzlies and American robins singing in the trees. The mosquitoes were waking too, so I was soon packed and on the trail for what was a wonderful day in spectacular scenery – a landscape in fact for which any superlatives are inadequate. The ascent to Stoney Indian Pass was just marvellous. Fantastic rock peaks, huge waterfalls, lovely lakes, beautiful flowers and bright, warm sunshine; perfect in fact. The trail climbed through a series of bowls to the pass, the forest now just a few clumps of stunted subalpine fir, where there was a glorious view down to Stoney Indian Lake. When my eyes dropped from the mountains it was to the mass of colours of the flowers in the meadows – glacier lily, paint brush, forget-me-not, potentilla, bear grass and many more. Just below the pass I found my first bear sign – a fresh paw mark superimposed on a hiker's boot print. The print was in soft mud but it looked like it was made by a grizzly rather than a black bear. There was no other sign of a bear though and other hikers were arriving on the pass from both directions. I guessed the bear was long gone from the trail, maybe up into the brush and boulders above the pass from where it could look down on the people milling about. I lingered on the pass for an hour, delighting in the landscape and only starting down when clouds began to form and the thunderstorm of two days before came to mind.

I was back down in thick forest and dense undergrowth when the rain began, this time unaccompanied by thunder and lightning. The

Continental Divide Trail sign in Glacier National Park

Waterton Valley Trail led to Goat Haunt at the head of Waterton Lake where I had checked in with the rangers on my Continental Divide Trail walk. After only one night in the wilderness I was surprised at how shocked I felt at the place with its buildings, paved paths and boat dock. There were no tent sites, just open-fronted, concrete-floored shelters. These kept the rain off but not the mosquitoes so I erected my mesh inner tent by tying guylines to hooks in the walls and round the front pillar of the shelter. It didn't look nice but then neither did the utilitarian shelter block. Nearby a bear warning notice had the word 'bear' crossed out and 'lion' added, saying it was frequenting the developed areas. Out on the lake a common loon (great northern diver in Britain) swam slowly past, a magnificent wild bird. Through thin clouds mountains came and went in the evening light. It was a superb setting despite the developments.

Glacier National Park and Canada's Waterton Lakes National Park make up the Waterton-Glacier International Peace Park, as announced on the large International Peace Park Pavilion at Goat Haunt. Two other hikers had lit a fire in the huge fireplace inside the pavilion and I joined them for an evening of trail talk. They were only here for a few days but had met when both were hiking the

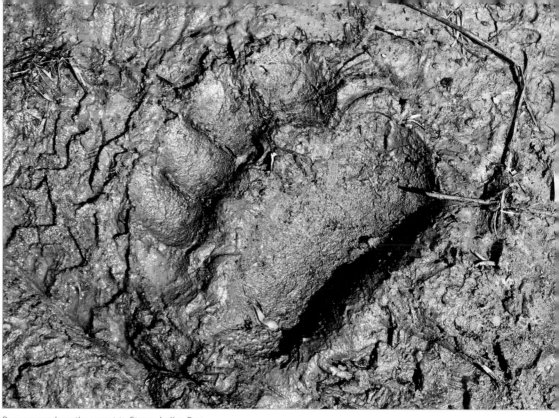

Bear pawmark on the ascent to Stoney Indian Pass

Appalachian Trail, the original long distance trail in the Eastern USA.

Tourist boats run down the lake from Waterton Lakes townsite to Goat Haunt. Until the tightening of entry restrictions passports weren't required here and hikers could arrive from Canada on foot and tourists wander away from the boats without any hindrance. Now everyone leaving the boat has to show their passports and no one who isn't from Canada or the USA is allowed in. The hiker's shelter was on the far side of the border post, though still well inside the USA, and I had to show my passport and explain I hadn't come from Canada just to get back on the trail. There

wasn't much feeling of international peace around. Still, the landscape is wild and marvellous and the artificial line that says 'this is the USA' and 'this is Canada' is ignored by the trees and animals.

A ranger came and checked on me as I had breakfast in the food preparation area. 50% chance of rain, she said. The skies were grey as I climbed to Brown Pass. Here at 6255 feet/1906.5 metres I crossed the Continental Divide. Until now all the water had flowed east to the Atlantic. From the pass everything flowed to the Pacific. I was on the crest of the continent and my walk to the Pacific really had begun.

At Brown Pass I had the option of two routes. The wilder, higher one went over Boulder Pass and descended to a ford of the North Fork of the Flathead River. Having been advised that there was still snow on the steep slopes of Boulder Pass and that anyway the river was a raging torrent full of snowmelt I had already decided I would take the lower route down the Bowman Lake valley. The weather was to make this a wise decision. The views from Brown Pass were spectacular with the mountains matching their names – The Hawksbill, The Sentinel, Thunderbird Mountain, Boulder Peak. Across the head of the Bowman valley Hole-In-The-Wall Falls crashed down the steep slopes below

Boulder Pass. A cold south-west wind swept the pass and black clouds were pouring across the sky, dramatic and threatening. I didn't stop. The storm began just as I regained the forest with a sudden burst of ferocious rain that soaked me to the skin before I could don my waterproof clothing. Thunder cracked and banged all around and lightning flashed every few minutes. I plunged down through the sodden vegetation, scurrying across little meadows that felt frighteningly exposed and wading through knee-deep torrents that were probable just trickles a few hours earlier. The storm lasted six hours. Before it finished I'd reached my next campground on the shores of Bowman Lake. Others were already here, huddled under trees in their waterproofs. Canoes were drawn up on the shore. As soon as I stopped I felt cold. Disobeying the rules I found the last empty site and crouched under a tree while I stripped off my wet clothes and donned dry ones. Only then did I pitch the tent and hang my food. Lying in the tent under my quilt in dry wool and fleece clothing I soon warmed up, venturing out when the rain ceased for a late cold supper of tortillas and cheese – trying to find dry fuel for the stove seemed futile when everything was dripping. There was a beautiful soft light over the lake with gentle clouds drifting round the

peaks. A calm and peaceful end to a dramatic day.

Over breakfast I spoke to two of the canoeists who had come up the lake the day before with their daughter, who looked about seven years old and was wandering about the campground in pink pyjamas and a fleece jacket. They'd had a rough time on the lake in the storm and were heading out. The park may be organised and to some extent sanitised but the wildness is still there, only just behind the well-made trails, neatly laid-out campgrounds and detailed signposts.

My walk was changing on this its fourth day as I was heading out of the park into country with few of its facilities. The high passes of Glacier were behind me now and there was just a walk beside Bowman Lake to the park boundary and then a descent through woods to the broad Flathead Valley. It looked like being a quiet day and one to reflect on the walk so far. But then as I ambled down the trail I saw two familiar figures coming towards me. Kris and Leanne! Having discovered my stove fuel in the van they'd decided to drive up the Flathead Valley and then hike in, hoping to meet me. So it was conversation rather than reflection that accompanied me to the trailhead.

Here I let Kris and Leanne take my pack and drive it down the road to the remote little settlement

Cruise boat on Upper Waterton Lakes

View from Brown Pass over the Bowman Valley to the approaching storm

long walk down the road to this bridge.

Polebridge is a tiny cluster of buildings centred round the amazing Polebridge Mercantile, which sells groceries, coffee and delicious home-baked goods. I found Kris and Leanne sitting outside the Mercantile and joined them for a welcome coffee and feta scone. The road walk had been hot and dusty and for the first time on the walk I was footsore. Down the road from the Mercantile was the North Fork Hostel, where Kris and Leanne had stayed the previous night. Here I pitched my tent, dried, along with the rest of my gear, by Kris and Leanne who had spread it out in the sun. Next to my little shelter was a huge tipi. Inside the hostel, which has no electricity (nowhere in Polebridge has mains electricity), just propane and kerosene for power, outdoor curios, many of them to do with skiing, were all around, along with books and quotes, including some from one of my favourites, Edward Abbey. Any place with Abbey quotes instantly endears itself to me! Oliver, the hostelmeister, gave me some advice as to routes in the days to come in the dark wooded hills of the Whitefish Range that I could see across the valley.

Kris and Leanne said farewell and headed back down the valley. They were returning to Issaquah the next day. I really wouldn't see them again for

of Polebridge while I walked, unburdened, down the gravel road. The forest here had been destroyed in a big fire with many blackened dead trees still standing. The fire wasn't recent though, as there was much regeneration. If I was at home in the Cairngorms these trees would be about 25 years old I thought. At the Polebridge ranger station I discovered the same applied here, the fire having been 22 years ago in 1988. As well as the forest, the fire destroyed the original pole bridge over the North Fork of the Flathead River. Crossing on a new bridge I looked down at the deep swirling water and knew I'd made the right decision not to take the alternative route. Unable to ford I'd have had a

many weeks. I had stove fuel now but tonight I didn't need it. Instead I dined in the North Fork Saloon on a delicious veggie pizza. Even after only three days of trail food I relished it. After the meal I sat outside and had a few beers with a bunch of firefighters from Texas whom I'd met briefly at the Bowman Lake campground. For some this had been their first backpacking trip and the weather had made it quite exciting. Other people gathered in the late sunshine and a few produced instruments. Soon there was an impromptu concert with violin, accordion and guitar and some excellent vocals. The musicians covered everything from Vivaldi to the Beatles and played really well. Afterwards I talked to Mary, the violinist, and was amazed when she said she didn't know most of the tunes as she came from a classical background.

Leaving Polebridge proved hard. The peaceful ambience of the place attracted me – as did the baking at the Mercantile where I had breakfast. The day was very hot too, which didn't encourage striding out. I think, too, there was a degree of trepidation as I knew the walk was about to become more challenging. Crossing Glacier National Park had been an easy break-in period, getting me used to hiking every day and camping every night and letting me gently into the mindset needed for a

long walk. Now I knew the trail signs, wide paths, prepared campgrounds and ranger patrols would be gone. The land ahead was less tamed, less frequented and more challenging even though the summits were lower and mostly wooded. The real nature of the Pacific Northwest Trail was about to be revealed. I hoped I could handle it.

After purchasing groceries in the Mercantile, which had just enough suitable items for the next few days, I couldn't think of any other reasons to stay so I left the delightful little hamlet behind and headed towards the rolling Whitefish hills. As I left the town I passed a hand-written sign reading 'Slow Down People Breathing'. When the first truck

Mountain lion warning at Goat Haunt – where I was camping

roared past on the dirt road sending up clouds of choking dust I understood. At the 'main' road in the valley, still unpaved, a sign read 'Canada 22 miles', the first of many reminders that the border was never far away. In the other direction the sign pointed to 'Columbia Falls 35 miles', a confirmation that Polebridge really was a long way from anywhere. That the road is unpaved is due mainly to the wishes of locals who wish to preserve their solitude and fear that a paved road would bring developments and too many people.

Across the valley a forest road led up through the woods above Hay Creek, eventually becoming the Hay Creek Trail. All around were steep, densely forested hills. At times, looking back, I could see the rock peaks of Glacier National Park. The trees were mostly conifers, tall and dark, with much undergrowth below them. This was a natural forest, not a plantation.

I'd intended camping at Hay Lake, which was marked as just off the trail, but somehow I went right past it and found myself on a good recently maintained trail that cut across a steep hillside. As there was no water or anywhere to camp I kept going. A dirt road appeared with a sign pointing to Red Meadow Lake. It was nearly a mile off-route but it did mean water so up the road I went to find a rough campground with a few tents and RVs situated on a narrow strip of land between two small lakes. Although beside a road there was none of the neatness and careful organisation of the backcountry campgrounds in Glacier National Park. I pitched my tent on a knoll above the lakes and was soon asleep, tired after 22 miles/35 kilometres on a very hot day.

"We're up here from Columbia Falls to escape the heat. It's 90°F down there" two other campers told me the next day. This heat, they said, was most unusual as had been the big storm two days previously, during which I'd descended to Bowman Lake, which had brought down trees in the towns

Western toad in the undergrowth beside Bowman Lake

of Kalispell and Whitefish. Less than a week on the trail and I'd already had an out of the ordinary storm and an out of the ordinary heatwave. Above the larger of the two lakes stood steep Red Meadow Peak with an obvious wide avalanche slope full of small shrubs running down to the lake between the trees. Four years earlier I was told, a huge avalanche had swept down that slope and blasted water, ice and fish out of the lake and up the other side, killing two snowmobilers. Grayling were left hanging in the trees afterwards, said my informant. The campers at the lake were here for fishing and relaxing. None were hikers. As I turned away from the lake a great blue heron flapped overhead, its long legs dangling below it, and settled onto a tree top.

Back *en route* I followed the splendid Whitefish Divide Trail, which wound along a ridgeline with fine views of deep valleys and steep wooded hills, many with craggy faces. Lining much of the trail was a mass of flowers in blue, red, yellow and white – paintbrush, gentian, pasque flowers and others. Elsewhere the terrain was stony with splintered rocks and boulders. Like the mountains in Glacier the hills here were built of sedimentary rock carved by ice. However, the landscape was very different to that of Glacier,

Mist and drifting clouds at Upper Bowmont Lake the morning after the storm

the hills much less rocky and mountainous, but somehow feeling more rugged and remote, partly due to the fact that I met nobody, as had been the case on the previous day's walk, but mainly due to the lack of any developments and amenities for hikers other than the narrow trails. There was no sign at the start of the trail and the dirt road

leading to it had a different number to that on my maps and notes. I would have to pay attention to navigation now. The trail was a mix of closed forest roads that were slowly growing over, narrow but reasonably maintained trails and old overgrown trails with many blow-downs – trees that had come down in storms – across them that I had to

clamber over. In places the trails almost faded away and were hard to follow. Small cairns marked the route in these places. Paying attention to the route, dealing with the fallen trees and looking for cairns all made hiking here more intense and involved than in Glacier. There I felt it would be hard to go wrong and the mostly smooth trails made for easy walking. Here going wrong would be all too easy and the trails were much more rough and rugged.

This being a ridge walk there was no water and in the hot sun I soon became very thirsty, especially during steep climbs, of which there were several. A small pond was marked on the map not far from the trail so I bushwhacked through a tangle of undergrowth and fallen trees to it, thinking I would camp there. But the pond was shallow and humming with mosquitoes and the shores were marshy and overgrown. I filled my water containers, waved away the bugs and scrabbled my way back to the trail. Half a mile further along I found an old, mostly overgrown, campsite with an ancient fire pit and some decaying cut logs. This would do for the night. With no sign of rain and barely a cloud in the sky I didn't need the tent. I did pitch the mesh inner though, as there were some mosquitoes buzzing around. During this hot, dry part of the walk having a mesh shelter proved invaluable as it was much cooler than a solid tent but still kept out insects. I could lie inside and watch the stars too and see any creatures that passed by so I felt less cut-off from the world than inside a full tent. I set up my kitchen on a log not far from my shelter.

As it appeared that this was a site where no-one had camped for a very long time and so not anywhere animals would expect to find human foodstuffs I didn't bother hanging my food but just placed it on the ground where I could see it from the tent. I had seen bear and coyote scat (dung) on the trail but none near this site. If there had been any I would have either moved on or hung my food high in the trees. However the thin trees with their

Artist's Fungus in the Bowman Lake woods

short, down-curved branches didn't look suitable for hanging food anyway, unless I strung a line between two of them, a difficult procedure with just one person. I knew anyway that the likelihood of a bear visiting my camp or showing interest in my food was slight. In less frequented places like this bears are truly wild and usually avoid people. I wasn't sending out strong smells either – no frying bacon or strong cheese. My dried food was sealed in plastic bags that should keep in most of the smells and these were then packed in an Ursack, a very tough stuffsack made from 'bullet proof' fabric and said to be bear proof. I looped the Ursack drawcord round a small tree, though I suspected a determined bear could easily have uprooted the latter and run off with it and the stuffsack.

Of the two species of bear found in the USA the grizzly is potentially the most dangerous if disturbed. However even in places with many bears and many people like Glacier National Park bear encounters resulting in injury or death are extremely rare. In the 1800s there were probably around 50,000 grizzlies in the Western USA. Today it's estimated there are only 1200-1400 left, all in the Northwestern States. 400 of these are in the Northern Continental Divide Ecosystem, mainly Glacier National Park, and 500 in the Yellowstone area further south in the Rockies. There were maybe 100 in the mountains I would cross in the next few weeks and then none until I reached the Cascades, where there might be 20 or so. Having not seen one in Glacier I was unlikely to even see a grizzly, let alone have a dangerous encounter with one. It was quite possible that there weren't actually any grizzlies in these mountains at all. That didn't mean dispensing with precautions of course and I was careful to note any bear sign and to ensure any bears would know of my presence in places where they were unlikely to see, hear or smell me. I hadn't forgotten my first meeting with a grizzly on a walk the length of the Canadian Rockies, where there are far more grizzlies than in the USA. I was hiking up a timberline trail in the rain with the wind in my face and a noisy creek below me to one side, just the conditions where a bear wouldn't realise I was there. A movement caught my eye and I glanced across the creek to see a huge pale-coloured grizzly coming towards me. It was a few hundred feet away and had its head down. Initially I was thrilled and excited at seeing my first grizzly but my feelings almost immediately changed to fear as the bear was quickly coming closer. If it suddenly noticed me at close quarters it might decide I was a threat and attack so I needed to attract its attention, which I did by jumping up and down, shouting, clapping my hands and blowing my safety whistle. The bear stopped then raised its head and moved it from side to side as if trying to locate the source of the noise or catch a scent. Then it turned aside and headed off down the creek, leaving me feeling extremely relieved. I would be more alert in future.

Because there are so few grizzlies left they are protected and the U.S. Fish and Wildlife Service has a Grizzly Bear Recovery Program (http://www.fws.gov/mountain-prairie/species/mammals/grizzly/). Keeping humans and bears apart is important for the grizzlies as well as us. Bears that attack people are usually shot and this is often the fate of any that become used to raiding camps or houses for food.

Black bears are far more common than grizzlies and are found in most wild areas of the USA. The estimated population is 300,000. They are most likely to run away on seeing a person. However in some popular areas like the High Sierra of California they have become used to raiding campgrounds for food, though attacks on people are very unusual. In the remoter environs of most of the Pacific Northwest Trail black bears were unlikely to be a problem. I'd seen black bears quite

a few times on previous walks and in every case they'd run away.

The presence of predators that can kill you is a strong indicator of true wilderness. Without large wild areas there would be no wild bears. Being wary of them and behaving sensibly in their country is wise. But there is a danger of over-estimating the threat and under-estimating much more likely hazards. I knew that getting lost, hypothermia, heatstroke, an incapacitating injury far from help, drowning in a creek and being struck by lightning were all far more likely than being injured by a bear and none of them were very likely anyway. In fact I was to find that the biggest danger and one I was exposed to for longest didn't come in wild places but on highways where I was in constant danger from high-speed vehicles.

With thoughts of bears far from my mind I sat back against a log with a hot drink and looked round my night's home. This is my first real wild camp, I thought – unplanned, no facilities and no permit needed. No one knew where I was. No ranger would come round to check on me. I was responsible for myself. Freedom!

A buzzing in the air distracted me. I gazed round and there were two tiny black-throated humming birds hovering in the air and displaying to each other. I watched them until they suddenly flashed off into the trees. Shortly afterwards a small hawk sped through the trees. I was alone, apart from the natural world.

A bright moon shone down through the trees as I zipped myself into the tent away from the mosquitoes. I spent some time tinkering with my spare camera, whose retractable lens had jammed open. Nothing I could do would get it working though. One week and one camera down. I hoped my other one would prove more durable.

The next night I was camped on a similar long-disused site complete with the remnants of an old campfire. This time there was water though

A contrast in camping styles, Polebridge

Polebridge Mercantile, home to delicious baking

as a creek ran near by. I was glad not to have carry water any distance as it had been another very hot day with much strenuous ascent and I was finding the unfamiliar and unexpected heat enervating. The effort was worthwhile however as the Whitefish Divide Trail took me over 7211 foot/2198 metre high Mount Locke whose summit gave tremendous views over the huge Whale Creek valley back to the now shrinking pointed peaks of Glacier National Park. Then it was down into the forest and a mix of trails and dirt roads on one of which I passed some vehicles and people, the first I'd seen since leaving Red Meadow Lake. On the trails there was much fresh bear scat but again none near my camp site. An osprey flew close overhead, a magnificent bird that reminded me of home and Loch Garten where ospreys returned to nest after years of absence due to persecution. Then I jumped as a grouse with chicks exploded out of the bushes in front of me and crashed off through the forest. Less attractive creatures were the big horseflies and little black flies that gave bites that I found more painful and irritating than those of mosquitoes.

In camp I examined my feet. They were red and sore. I'd already removed my socks and then the insoles from my shoes as the heat was making my feet swell and my shoes feel tight. All I could do

Impromptu concert, Polebridge

now was cool my feet with cold creek water.

I woke to the sound of tramping. Three people were passing my tent – at 7.30 in the morning! One had a hard hat so I guessed they were a trail maintenance crew. They were the first people I'd seen away from roads since leaving Glacier National Park three days before. In Glacier

I'd met dozens of hikers every day. So far I had met none here. A trailhead sign said that trails 341 and 85 were closed for maintenance, which was not very helpful as none of my maps showed trails with these numbers. I followed trails with other numbers up through the forest to 7203 foot/2195 metre high Mount Wam. An old white-painted fire

Road sign, Polebridge

lookout cabin stood on the top. Although a few are still in use most of these fire lookouts have been abandoned in favour of aircraft and satellite surveillance. Some have been removed, some are slowly decaying. However many, like the one on Mount Wam, are now available for holiday rental. Unlike many you can't drive to this lookout though but have to hike up. The idea of staying in a fire lookout on the summit of a mountain is romantic and of course they are located where there is a widespread view. I discovered fire lookouts many years ago through the novels of Jack Kerouac. In *The Dharma Bums* and *Desolation Angels* he describes working as fire watcher on Desolation Peak in the North Cascades, after being influenced by poet, conservationist and wilderness lover Gary Snyder, who appears lightly disguised in the novels as Japhy Ryder. Kerouac is best known for car journeys, hitch-hiking, jazz clubs and the Beat Generation of the 1950s but for me it was the Snyder influenced wilderness passages that had a big impact, even though I only had a hazy idea of where the places described were and my idea of wilderness was the English Lake District. Discovering who Ryder really was I went on to read Gray Snyder's poetry. Turning now to a forty-year old book, a collection called *A Range of Poems,* I open it to find the first poem

is called *Mid-August At Sourdough Mountain Lookout* and find lines that conjure up the solitude and sense of remoteness found when alone on a mountain top:

> I cannot remember things I once read
> A few friends, but they are in cities.
> Drinking cold snow-water from a tin cup
> Looking down for miles
> Through high still air.

Much later, after I'd discovered real wilderness, I read Edward Abbey's stories of being a fire lookout. Perhaps the most compelling and evocative writing is in Abbey's excellent novel *Black Sun*, based on the author's time as a fire lookout on the North Rim of the Grand Canyon, which is also covered factually in his equally excellent collection of essays *Abbey's Road*. In the Preface to *Black Sun* Abbey writes of lookouts 'A tower in the woods. Far away from all that sustains sanity' and in the essay *Fire Lookout* in *Abbey's Road* he says 'Men go mad in this line of work. Read a book called The Dharma Bums by Jack Kerouac and you'll see what I mean... Kerouac never recovered'. However, despite this negative outlook, Abbey's tales of his fire lookout work are mostly humorous and he also writes 'I spent four sweet summers on that sublime

North Rim'. Abbey's lookout wasn't remote though and he had plenty of visitors and went to the bar in the nearest village once a week. Kerouac's lookout was 15 miles/24 kilometres by foot or horse from the nearest road so working there really was a solitary existence. I don't agree with Abbey though. Kerouac's spiritual and emotional troubles long pre-dated his stay in the lookout. Indeed, it could be argued that he was more at peace far above the world of bars, cities and cars than in it and that his wilderness sojourn was beneficial rather than harmful. I've never spent a summer in one place in the wilderness, sitting atop a mountain watching the landscape. I imagine it could be restful and contemplative but also tedious, lonely and probably frustrating, with a feeling of being constrained and captive, tied to the lookout. The freedom of the wilds would be lost and I would resent that.

A breeze blew across the bare summit and distant views were hazy. The weather was changing. Closer to hand the world was one of forested hills and ridges and deep wooded valleys with just the occasional scree or rock slope to break up the green land. Away to the east the Glacier peaks were fainter now. The ground around the lookout was bright with flowers including penstemon, bear grass, purple eyed mariposa lily and paintbrush.

Lower Red Meadow Lake in the Whitefish Mountains

From the forest below I could hear the chainsaws of the trail crew.

Beyond Mount Wam lay the Ten Lakes Scenic Area, whose peaks, more rugged than any since Glacier, I could see from the summit. Continuing along the ridge the rocky pyramid of Stahl Peak with a distinctive cupola-like lookout on the summit stood out in the views. The guidebook suggested a horseshoe-shaped route right round the Scenic Area, a distance of 19 miles/30 kilometres, starting with a 5 mile/8 kilometres climb on a road. Or I could stay on the trail and cut straight across the open end of the horseshoe, which was just 2.6 miles/4 kilometres. The sky was darkening and my feet were sore. I took the shorter route, and was very glad I did as it was superb. Probably the best section of trail since Glacier in fact. Called the Highline Trail it ran right underneath the magnificent long east face of St Clair Peak, a real rock mountain, passing a lovely little lake and finishing with a narrow path across steep scree below rugged cliffs. The views of the Scenic Area were excellent but the thickening black clouds kept me moving. I was relishing being out of the trees but I also wanted to get back into them before the storm broke. I just made it, the first rumble of thunder occurring as I started a steep descent. Soon the thunder was almost continuous though there was no rain.

A different crashing sound had me staring into the trees. A beautiful cinnamon-coloured black bear emerged from the undergrowth, paused on a log to look at me and then bounded away uphill. The first bear of the walk. I hoped any others would be as timid. Watching it run away over rough ground covered with fallen branches I realised again why running away from a bear is a bad idea.

The descent was taking me down out of the hills into the next big valley. The high mountain trees – subalpine fir, Engelmann's spruce – were left behind and bigger trees appeared, including

Flower meadow along the Whitefish Divide Trail

some lovely western red cedar. I camped amongst massive ponderosa pines and Douglas firs not far from a creek. The ground under the trees was more open here than on the higher slopes where the trees were smaller and more closely packed. There were many blowdowns in the forest though and it took fifteen minutes to bushwhack to the creek for water.

I was now just 8 miles/13 kilometres from the little town of Eureka in the Tobacco Valley, which separated the Whitefish Range from the Purcell Mountains. A confusing mix of vague trails, dirt roads and paved roads led to the town, which I reached at the far end from the route described in the guidebook. Eureka was a typical Western American town – long and thin with most buildings on the main street which stretched for over 2 miles/3.2 kilometres. The Ksamba motel provided low cost accommodation and was just fifteen minutes walk from the post office and laundromat – two of the essentials in a town stop on a long distance walk. Having been out for nine days I decided on a rest day in Eureka. From experience I knew that after ten to fourteen days I started to run down if I didn't take some time off. As it was another eight days or so to the next town this seemed a good place to spend a day. Also, my

Taking in the view from the Whitefish Divide Trail

sore feet needed time off even if the rest of me was okay.

Eureka, which has a population of around 1,000, proved a friendly place with all the facilities I needed, including an organic grocery, good cafes and a few shops that sold books. In a western store, amongst the fancy saddles and cowboy boots, I found a book entitled *Sherlock Holmes the Montana Chronicles*. That I couldn't resist! My only complaint with Eureka was that it was too long. By the time I'd walked the length of it twice my feet were sore again. The hot weather showed no sign of breaking so a change of footwear was needed. Sandals would be ideal. Fortuitously, directly

opposite the motel was a Carhartt's store that sold outdoor gear. I found a pair of Merrell sandals on sale for $70. I thought of the sandals I had at home. I didn't need another pair. But right now I did so I bought them. That, I thought, would teach me to undertake a long distance walk with just one pair of footwear, something I had never done before.

In the motel I ate Subway rolls, drank soft drinks, checked and wrote emails, updated my Facebook page and my blog and wrote and emailed a piece for my backpacking column in TGO magazine, complete with photographs taken on my smartphone. My smartphone had now changed from a GPS and camera to a mini computer. It really was an astonishing device. I thought back to earlier long distance walks. On my first, from Land's End to John O'Groats in Britain, I had sent postcards to keep people informed as to my progress and the outdoor shop where I worked had moved a coloured pin along a map with my route marked. Then on the Pacific Crest Trail I had mailed hand written trip reports to the Pacific Crest Club and been amazed when copies of the club newsletter with them in appeared in my mail before I had finished the trail. Now my words could appear instantly and be read anywhere there was an internet connection. I felt surprised. I didn't feel in contact with home.

Downtown Eureka, Montana

Scotland was a far off, distant place. My mind was here in the Pacific Northwest, in this little town in the vastness of the great forests and mountains. No amount of electronic communications could take that away.

The great luxury of this town stop was not the Internet connection or the cafes or the soft bed though, but the simple pleasure of a bath, of slowly soaking in a tub of hot water.

On the Whitefish Divide Trail

CHAPTER 2

YAAK COUNTRY

THE PURCELL MOUNTAINS, EUREKA TO BONNERS FERRY
July 30 – August 6
95 miles/153km

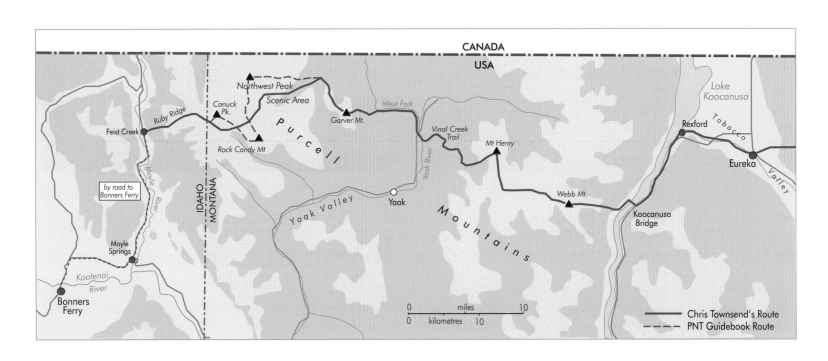

A Subway takeaway breakfast in the motel while I packed, then a second more leisurely breakfast in the excellent Shonduel's Organic Gourmet to Go Café set me up for leaving Eureka. My box was mailed to my next town. Spare maps went to Kris. My town chores were done. Now I had a day's walking to reach the mountains, mainly on the road beside the vast Lake Koocanusa reservoir, which is 90 miles/145 kilometres long and stretching far into Canada. A US/Canadian project, the reservoir was built to provide hydro-electric power and to control the Kootenai River, which flooded regularly. It was completed in 1972. The name comes from the first three letters of Kootenai and Canada plus USA.

Before the road walk I had a more pleasant amble beside the Tobacco River on an old railway line that had been turned into a trail. The river wound in gentle meanders through an open landscape of sandy bluffs and marshy meadows. With campgrounds, roads and farms this was pleasant countryside but not wild country. There was wildlife though with several ospreys flying over the river and one on its huge untidy nest atop an old power line pole plus my first bald eagle slowly flapping over the water. Soon the river was absorbed into an arm of the reservoir, on which I could see many jet skis and power boats, and the

The Tobacco River

trail passed through woods to the little settlement of Rexford. Here I had lunch in a café to fortify myself for the 7 mile/11 kilometre slog along a highway to the only bridge across the reservoir.

I passed the time on the hot road walk by reading *Sherlock Holmes: The Montana Chronicles*, which I found entertaining though not up to the

standard of the original stories. There was little traffic. Twice drivers stopped to offer me a lift. The first stopped in a parking place and waited for me. He was a hiker and was concerned the heat might affect me. However I had my trusty Tilley Hat to keep off the sun and had drunk a number of soft drinks in Rexford and was carrying plenty

of water. The second driver was heading the other way and did a U-turn on seeing me. 'I can take you across the bridge', he offered. I explained I was happy to walk, indeed wanted to walk, which must have seemed odd given the hot weather and not very interesting surroundings, the road being lined by dense conifers. Finally conceding that this mad Brit was going to continue walking he insisted that I accept a can of beer for when I reached camp. Feeling it would be ungracious to refuse I tucked the can into a pack pocket. I'd drink it that evening and the empty can wouldn't weigh much on the journey to the next town. My insistence on refusing a ride lay in the only rule I have for long distance walking, which is that I will walk every step of the way. I might leave the route to resupply, when any form of transport would be fine, but I would always return to the same spot to restart walking. I like the idea of creating a continuous line from start to finish. I also feel that if I took a ride once it would be easier to do so again and a walk could soon disintegrate into a series of disconnected trips linked by car journeys.

Crossing the Kookanusa Bridge took me into the southern end of the Purcell Mountains, most of which lie in Canada. These mountains are steeper and more rugged than the Whitefish Range and

Lake Kookanusa

quite remote and unfrequented. A roadside sign warned 'This is Grizzly Bear Habitat' and 'Hikers: be alert on trails'. In his guidebook Ron Strickland wrote 'this section will test your map and compass skills and your ability to deal with the uncertainties of primitive backcountry travel'. My first challenge was to obtain water. The guidebook said a creek

below the road near the trailhead was the last until after the ascent of 5988 foot/1825 metre Webb Mountain, a 3600 foot/1100 metre climb I wasn't intending to undertake until the next day. What the guidebook didn't say was that the descent to the creek was steep, loose and treacherous. It took 20 minutes and I needed hiking poles to keep my

Bear notice

feet. This was some of the trickiest terrain of the walk so far and all just below a highway. Water containers full, I hiked up the Webb Mountain Trail to the first flat area, on the edge of a little crag amongst ponderosa pines. This would be my first camp in the Purcells.

The night was warm, stuffy even, the air still and heavy. The sky was red at dawn and soon there was thunder and light rain, which had died away by the time I set off though the sky remained cloudy. The steep climb up Webb Mountain took nearly four hours. As I neared the top the long sinuous thread of Lake Kookanusa, shining between dark banks of conifers, appeared far below with the rolling wooded Whitefish Range beyond it. After the strenuous ascent I was a little disappointed to see a truck parked below a fine tall lookout tower, even though I knew from the map that a dirt road ran to the summit. A couple were in the lookout, which was available to rent from Kootenai National Forest. They used to hike, they told me, but now stayed in lookouts – fourteen so far. They'd seen much bear scat on the road. I'd seen none on the trail. They offered me a drink of water, which was welcome after the long sweaty climb as I had little left and didn't know how far the next source would be. From the lookout the forested hills undulated all

around. Another lookout was visible to the north-west on Mount Henry, the next summit on my walk and the high point between Lake Kookanusa and the Yaak Valley.

Happy to be back in the high country I followed forested trails round Thirsty Mountain to the twin Boulder Lakes, beyond which rose the broken cliffs of Boulder Mountain. There were several used camp sites round the lower lake with big fire-rings and half-burnt logs. In one fire-ring were some shiny cans, still with paper on. Someone had been here recently. Despite the damaged sites and litter it was a scenic spot and an ideal place to camp. Popular sites attract animals though and for the first time I was disturbed during the night by attempts to raid my food supplies. Not by a bear – I'd probably have lost my food if it had been – but by some much smaller mammal, probably a ground squirrel. After being woken a few times by the sound of scratching on my food bag I retrieved it and brought it into the tent porch. The Ursack was intact but did have a few tiny new tears.

A half-moon hung high in the blue sky at dawn while a westerly breeze swept across the lake, causing nice rippled reflections. Packing up I couldn't find the stuffsack for my pots. I'd left it with my kitchen gear, the rest of which was

still there though the lid had been knocked off a pot and other items scattered about. I could only presume the raiding animal had run off with it. As my pots were sooty I needed some sort of bag for them. Luckily, I still had the Glacier National Park plastic bag with the bear warnings on it, which I'd carried in case it came in useful. It did as a pot stuffsack for the rest of the walk.

From Boulder Lakes the trail wound over steep wooded hills to the base of Mount Henry. Mostly I was in dark conifer forest but there was occasional relief from little clearings full of flowers, especially bright blue lupins and bright red paintbrush, and glimpses of craggy hillsides. The west wind kept the air fresher and cooler than it had been for many days. The trails in the dense forest were faint in places and for the first time on the walk I missed a junction and continued down the wrong trail for half an hour or so, finally realising I'd gone wrong when the terrain dropped away instead of rising, as expected. The GPS mapping on my smartphone came in useful here as I was able to see exactly where I was, difficult with map and compass in a forest. The trails remained sketchy and I lost the one up the final stony cone of Mount Henry. The way was obvious however – up – so I took a direct cross-country route over loose rocky ground and

Looking back down to Lake Kookanusa from high on Webb Mountain

through little groves of gnarled western white pine and stunted subalpine fir. As I clambered over the rocks I felt a touch of excitement at being off trail and almost out of the trees. Cross-country route-finding is always more intense than following a trail, especially in rugged terrain. You have to concentrate on the ground immediately in front of you, choosing where to place your feet, whether to scramble over or go round boulders and watching for loose rocks and adjusting your balance when you step on one, as inevitably happens, while at the same time looking ahead to pick out the best way to go and to avoid being pushed off the direction you want. Without care it's very easy to keep taking the less demanding way and slowly turning from the right direction. Do this for long enough and you can end up heading in the opposite way to the one you thought you were taking. Finding a way like this is satisfying and challenging. The final climb up 7234 foot/2004 metre Mount Henry was only a brief taste of off-trail travel, and it would have been hard to go wrong, but it was enjoyable none the less.

An old unlocked lookout tower stood on the bare rocky summit. Green wooded hills rippled all around, stretching out to the horizon. Back east I could see, faint and distant now, the jagged peaks of Glacier National Park. A cold wind swept the summit. Big clouds were building up and I'd heard thunder earlier so I didn't stay long on the peak but was soon heading down the loose splintered rocks to the shelter of the trees. I descended on the Spring Trail. The guidebook mentioned this as part of the ascent route – and described the spring itself as having 'some of the best and most welcome water on the PNT' – but somehow I'd missed it. I needed to find the spring itself though as my water bottles had been empty for several hours and there'd been no water for quite a while. I was already thirsty and if the map was correct and there was no water for the next four miles or so I would soon be extremely thirsty if I couldn't find it. Happily, although half-hidden in vegetation the tiny spring was easy to find. It was covered by a wooden board with the words "keep lid on" engraved on it and an old ceramic coffee pot on top. I lifted these aside and looked down into a small stone-lined hole. It was dry. Not far below the spring though was a small pool. The water was clear and tasted fine. I drank copiously then filled my water bottles and set off down the trail.

After a little more time had been spent backtracking when I missed another faint trail junction I settled into a long descent on the Vinal Creek Trail, much of it in an old burned area from which I could look back to Mount Henry. A new forest was regenerating in the burn with many young trees ranging from one foot to twenty feet/0.3 to 6 metres tall. After nearly four thousand feet/1220 metres of descent I reached Vinal Creek, set in a steep-sided narrow valley. The trail ran alongside some beaver ponds to Turner Creek Falls, a lovely thin waterfall dropping straight down a rocky chasm onto boulders where it fanned out and tumbled into a pool through a big log jam. A beautiful spot but I needed somewhere to camp and there was little flat ground. Just before the falls I'd passed a flattened area of vegetation where I guessed someone else had camped recently, possibly another PNT hiker. There was just room to squeeze my tent in amongst the lush foliage. The day had been tough and I was tired. I'd only hiked 11 miles/18 kilometres but it had taken me 11 hours, due to the route-finding difficulties and the huge amount of ascent. I wanted to sleep straight away but knew that if I did so without eating I'd wake hungry in the middle of the night. This is where dried food that just requires the addition of hot water is useful. I'd bought some packets of Idahoan instant potato in Polebridge. It was time to eat one. I added some cheese for extra calories

One of the Boulder Lakes, Purcell Mountains

and found it quite tasty. On the packet it said 'best before Nov 2009' but being eight months out of date didn't seem to have affected it. Having eaten I fell asleep and didn't wake for nine hours.

With big rock walls, beaver dams and lovely western red cedars, their deeply furrowed deep red fibrous bark glowing in the sun, the Vinal Creek valley was impressive. Soon after leaving my camp I reached Fish Lakes, where I found many camp sites with log tables and benches and a rather depressing amount of plastic and foil scattered around, some of which I collected and stowed in my pack. Whilst there was plenty of space here I preferred my little spot amongst the bushes. After Vinal Creek I was mostly in deep forest all day, though with some views from burned areas. There was thunder in the air and the distant hills were hazy. Light rain fell briefly, just enough to soak the vegetation along the narrow trail and ensure wet feet and legs as I brushed past. Rather than landscapes the day was one for wild life and impressive trees. As I climbed away from the creek two mule deer bucks with new antlers in velvet watched me from a clearing. A pair of ravens whirled overhead and then a red-tailed hawk floated past, its call reminiscent of the buzzards of home, which are a close relative. In the old burned and logged areas there was much tall

pink fireweed, which springs up readily in disturbed ground. I sweated up the trail from the creek in the humid air, my thermometer recording 25.5°C/80°F. The trail was dry and firm but deep grooves from horse's hooves showed how soft it would be after rain. A trail crew had been through recently as there were many cut logs, showing that I would

have had many blow-downs to clamber over not many days earlier. Again the trail faded away into nothingness in places, especially more open areas, but this time its line was marked by small cairns, sometimes no more than one rock atop another. I added stones to some of the latter.

On the descent to the Yaak River I hiked

The spring on Mount Henry

through some of the most splendid big trees I had yet seen on the walk – western red cedar, Douglas fir and western larch; magnificent old growth trees, redolent of wilderness and a complex ecosystem. Crossing the Yaak Valley I passed a reedy pool where a belted kingfisher, an exotic-looking blue and white bird with a tall shaggy crest on its head, was sitting on a branch while a tall great blue heron, looking much like the grey heron of home, stood in the edge of the water. From the Yaak Valley Forest Service roads led back up into the hills and over to the West Fork of the Yaak River. A few vehicles passed me but mostly the dusty roads were quiet. I read most of the time, distracted occasionally by birds and once by an American badger, squatter and lower built than British badgers but with some similarities, especially the striped face (both are members of the weasel family). The badger peered at me as I approached and then disappeared down a culvert. I camped beside the road close to the West Fork, a utilitarian site.

The Yaak Valley and surrounding area is very remote. Few people live here and few visit. Yet it has become known through the work of writer and conservationist Rick Bass, who lives here and has written extensively about the area and led campaigns to save what has not yet been logged

from destruction. I did not know his writing about this area when I hiked through it, though I recognised his name from a mention in the PNT guidebook as I had a book of his, *The Lost Grizzlies*, about searching for any last grizzlies in the San Juan mountains of Colorado far to the south. I was to pick up one of his books about the Yaak, *Winter*, at my next town stop and then read perhaps the key one, *The Book of Yaak*, after the walk was finished. The little settlement of Yaak was seven miles/11 kilometres off my route, so, not needing to resupply, I didn't visit it. If I'd already read Bass's Yaak books I would have done, if only to visit the Dirty Shame Saloon and the Yaak Mercantile, which feature in his writings.

As it was, reading Rick Bass on the Yaak, on his falling in love with the place and then his realisation that it was threatened and that he wanted, or rather felt impelled, to do something about it and had to get involved in campaigning to do so brought back many memories and I could relate directly to his experience even though mine was based in the faraway Scottish Highlands. Here I had lost my innocence regarding wild land and gained a knowledge that was both revelatory and dismaying. When I first visited the Highlands I thought it a huge unspoilt magnificent wilderness.

Turner Creek Falls, Purcell Mountains

I assumed the landscape and wildlife were mostly untouched by human hand. Then I made the mistake of reading about my new passion and discovered

Beaver ponds on Vinal Creek

that it was damaged and the damage was still continuing. Words like 'degraded' and phrases like 'wet desert' shook me. I came to understood that much of the natural forest had been destroyed and that sheep and deer, whose natural predators had been exterminated, prevented any regeneration. Most of the forests I saw were plantations, mostly of Sitka spruce, now the commonest tree in Scotland (and ironically one I would see in its natural habitat towards the end of the walk and one 'discovered' by Scots plant collector David Douglas, who I was to read about later in the walk). Then there were the bulldozed roads and ski resorts (and latterly wind turbines). The remaining wildness in the Highlands was shrinking fast. Once I knew this and could see the signs I couldn't ignore it. Like Bass with the Yaak I had no option but to work to protect it, even though that has meant long, often tedious, meetings, committees, endless strings of emails, badly written bureaucratic reports and documents stuffed full of ugly jargon. Plus especially the frustration of trying to get through to politicians who, even if they represent the Highlands, seemed purely concerned with economic growth and development with no feeling for the land or wildlife and always quoted jobs and money as justification for anything. One politician accused me of nimbyism for objecting to a wind farm on the Isle of Skye, which is over 100 miles/160 kilometres from my home. I quite liked the idea of having such a huge backyard! Reading Rick Bass on the Yaak gives the lie to the charge of nimbyism, a lazy way of dismissing those who care about places. If someone who lives in and loves a place cannot speak up in its defence then who can?

Bass says of the Yaak 'the rain lashes against the mountains, the forest types merge with one another – the Pacific Northwest mixing with the northern Rockies to make new and unique forms of diversity – and what comes from all this cataclysm is the deepest wildness'. The area has a complete range

Fish Lakes, Vinal Creek valley

of wildlife though only just – maybe ten to thirty grizzlies and an even smaller number of wolves that pass through occasionally. Just passing through myself I could only touch on the majesty and richness of the area. Bass, who has lived here many years, knows it intimately and describes it eloquently in his books, in the tradition of John Muir and the High Sierra and Edward Abbey and the Southwest deserts. Yet whilst he is writing about one small corner of Montana his words apply to anywhere that wildness is under threat. 'You cannot measure the magic of a forest, or the effect a healthy, growing wild place has on your spirit'. Indeed, you cannot.

Bass's writings are more about the nature of the Yaak and his experience of it than about campaigning to save it. He revels in the natural world and his encounters with animals, trees, snow and every aspect of it. This is important for conservationists. It is too easy to move away from such roots and lose contact with what environmentalism should be about. Some 'environmental' groups that started out as defenders of nature and wilderness have become more concerned with defending industry and development. I think of them as urban environmentalists who have lost contact with the wild. The people who founded these groups long ago, such as David Brower, (who founded Friends of

the Earth amongst other groups), would be shocked to hear them campaigning for the destruction of wild land in Scotland by building wind farms and the despoliation of the deserts of California with vast arrays of solar panels. When thinking of the dangers of this disconnection I always remember two of my favourite quotations:

'Keep close to Nature's heart... and break clear away, once in awhile, and climb a mountain or spend a week in the woods. Wash your spirit clean'. John Muir.

'A thing is right when it tends to preserve the integrity, stability and beauty of the biotic community. It is wrong when it tends otherwise'. Aldo Leopold.

Applying Aldo Leopold's statement, known as his land ethic, shows that logging the Yaak or building wind farms on Scottish hills are wrong, both 'tend otherwise'. Reminding oneself of the beauty of nature and the joy of being in the wilds, as Muir advises, is a way to restore one's spirits and strength as well as a reminder of why all the dull campaigning work (which both Muir and Leopold undertook) is necessary. As he was wont to do Edward Abbey put it more forcefully:

'Do not burn yourself out. Be as I am–a reluctant enthusiast... a part time crusader, a half-

hearted fanatic. Save the other half of yourselves and your lives for pleasure and adventure. It is not enough to fight for the land; it is even more important to enjoy it. While you can. While it is still there. So get out there and mess around with your friends, ramble out yonder and explore the forests, encounter the *grizz*, climb the mountains. Run the rivers, breathe deep of that yet sweet and lucid air, sit quietly for a while and contemplate the precious stillness, that lovely, mysterious and awesome space. Enjoy yourselves, keep your brain in your head and your head firmly attached to your body, the body active and alive, and I promise you this much: I promise you this one sweet victory over our enemies, over those deskbound people with their hearts in a safe deposit box and their eyes hypnotized by desk calculators. I promise you this: you will outlive the bastards'.

These thoughts were far from mind at my roadside camp in Yaak Country. I had broken clear away and was out there enjoying it. Perhaps, though, just hiking the Pacific Northwest Trail is helping the conservation of the areas it passes through. A trail can become a campaigning tool and now that the PNT is a National Scenic Trail there are strong reasons for conserving and restoring the lands through which it passes. Otherwise that

word 'scenic' becomes a mockery. Every hiker who travels the trail, whether for a day or a summer, can become a defender of its environs, another voice to speak for the protection of the wild.

As the first daylight trickled through the trees I was woken by the harsh cries of a raven circling somewhere above and a squirrel chattering in a nearby tree. I'd grown used to the dry air and was surprised to find the tent outer soaked inside and out and a heavy dew on the ground. The relative humidity was 100%. The sky above was clear but the sun had still to filter through the trees and the air was damp and chilly and when the sun came it was hazy and dull. Clouds soon replaced it. I read my way through the morning as I tramped eight miles/13 kilometres on forest roads to the start of the Garver Mountain Trail. Hazy hills appeared through gaps in the forest. Once a long-tailed weasel ran across the road with something in its jaws but overall my book was more interesting than the forest, which was broken and scabby with regenerating clear-cuts. The Garver Mountain Trail required a little more concentration so the book went away for the climb to the 5874 foot/1790 metre peak. The summit area was rocky and quite extensive with a big lookout tower, a log cabin and an outhouse. The dark cloudy sky meant distant

views were faint and there was a chill breeze so I was soon heading back down into the forest. In fact the views from the trail were better than those from the summit as it crossed several open rocky slopes and I could look ahead to the peaks of the Northwest Peak Scenic Area, some with snow patches on their flanks. Then the day ended with more forest road walking and another roadside camp by the West Fork of the Yaak River, which had made a huge loop to the north while I'd cut straight across the hills. A truck clattered past in a cloud of dust, the second of the day. On the trails there was no-one. I hadn't seen another hiker since leaving Glacier National Park ten days before. Just before camp I passed big, marshy, Pete's Creek Meadows, a lovely expanse of lush grasses, and realised that it wasn't just hikers I wasn't seeing. There had also been a lack of meadows since Glacier as the hills were all steep-sided and the valleys narrow.

After a couple of not so interesting days – I hesitate to use the word dull though I may have thought it – I woke feeling excited as ahead lay the first long above timberline section since Glacier National Park in the Northwest Peak Scenic Area. I was pleased to see the sky was clear and the sun bright. It hadn't reached camp though and I breakfasted wearing my wool hat and down jacket.

I drank plenty of spiced apple cider and coffee/hot chocolate mix and then filled my water bottles as it looked as though there might be no water for many miles and there was much climbing to be done. I had a choice of routes – a northern loop described in Ron Strickland's original guidebook and a southern one outlined very briefly in the new guidebook notes Li Brannfors had sent me. Both involved cross-country sections. Studying the map I found that I had already made a decision as I'd walked past the start of the northern route the previous day and was already a short way along the southern one. I would continue that way.

The day was tough with hard route finding and rugged terrain but my excitement was justified as the reward was the best scenery since Glacier. I left the road on the ominously named Midge Creek Trail (anyone familiar with the Scottish Highlands will be unable to resist a shudder at the word 'midge' as clouds of these tiny biting insects plague the hills throughout the summer) and soon crossed a little stream – so much for carrying water from camp. The map showed the trail making a right angle turn. I walked straight past on a straight clear trail that wasn't on the map, only realising I'd missed the turn when I began a long descent in the wrong direction. I backtracked and started

Mountain scenery in the Yaak River country, Purcell Mountains

Checking the map, Yaak River country, Purcell Mountains

descending the way I'd come up. I'd missed it again. I'd been using my compass to check the direction. It wouldn't show me where the junction was though so I switched on the smartphone and used the GPS, following myself on the screen map until I stood at the start of the trail I needed to follow. There was no sign of it. I set off in the right direction, still using the GPS, and sure enough a sketchy trail eventually appeared.

Soon I was leaving the trees at the top of a wonderful rocky bowl with soaring ridges above me. The trail was hard to follow but it didn't matter here as the route ahead was clear anyway. Navigation is much easier on open mountainsides than in the forest. I rounded the deep bowl to a col below Rock Candy Mountain (I didn't know mountains were really called this – I only knew the name from Big Rock Candy Mountain, a silly children's song by Burl Ives I remembered from my childhood). The trail vanished completely here and I went cross-country along a fine rough ridge for a mile or so and then descended steep boulders back into the forest. All around lay rocky peaks and ridges, an inspiring vista. Back in the trees a good trail appeared and led through open subalpine forest with masses of bright flowers and superb views to 6934 foot/2113 metre Canuck Peak on the border between Montana and Idaho. I was about to enter my second state. Back down in the forest I had my first camp in Idaho at the head of Canuck Creek where boardwalks ran across the top of a small wet meadow. A tiny dry spot next to the boardwalk was just big enough for the tent.

The next night I was in a hotel in the little town of Bonners Ferry, a little to my surprise. This was my next supply point but didn't lie directly on the route so I was either going to have to find a ride or else walk some 16 miles/26 kilometres on a highway, which I really didn't want to do. Twice I would cross roads that led to the town. I decided that if I could find a lift I would take the first one.

If not I would walk on to the second. First I had to cross Ruby Ridge, a good trail walk with open views of surrounding hills. The day was hot and grew hotter as I dropped down through lovely forest to the Moyie River and the first road. There was no traffic and I was unsure what to do. Then a car passed and without thinking I stuck out a thumb. It stopped. The driver was very helpful. He wasn't going anywhere near Bonners Ferry but took me the short distance to the Feist Creek restaurant and bar that lay just north of where the trail I would take next left the road. I'd have walked here if I'd known it existed, as I imagine every PNT hiker would, but it wasn't mentioned in either the old guidebook or the new notes. The bar staff were surprised to see a hiker and were very helpful, letting me use their phone to call a taxi. There was no reply. Then Jessica, one of the staff, said she could take me most of the way but I'd have to wait a couple of hours until her shift finished. I settled down at the bar with a beer. One of the few other customers came over to chat. L.D.Huggins – just call me LD – was a local carpenter and builder. He worked all over the area, maintaining properties and building new ones and told me what a friendly and relaxing place this was to live. We toasted my walk and he gave me his business card – 'in case you need a

builder'. Then Jessica took me down the highway to an hour's walk from Bonners Ferry, an unpleasant hour as it was very hot and the road was busy.

Bonners Ferry was another long strung-out town, despite only having a population of around 2,500. The old centre was down by the Kootenai River, across which a ferry was established in 1864

by Edwin Bonner to take gold rush prospectors across the river as they headed north on the Wildhorse Trail to the East Kootenays in British Columbia where gold had been discovered. Now a big highway bridge spans the river and the town has spread out up the hillside alongside the main road. With mines nearby and masses of timber Bonners

Trail signs, Purcell Mountains

Along the Ruby Ridge Trail, Purcell Mountains

Ferry quickly grew. A steamer service began in 1883 and the first railway arrived in 1892. Farms sprang up on the rich land alongside the river. The old brick-built town centre is attractive and has architectural integrity. The newer sprawl along the highway is a confused mix of utilitarian modern buildings and more traditional-looking wooden ones.

Arriving hot, footsore and late I checked into the first accommodation I found, the Best Western Kootenai River Inn, which appeared to be as much a casino as a hotel with a huge room full of slot machines. A notice in my room said there were 500 machines and the casino was open 24 hours a day. I had no intention of gambling, the

room was expensive enough. It was cool though and had a shower, plus a giant television, which felt quite alien. I lay on the bed and stared at the ceiling. Stage two of my walk was over. I'd been out seventeen days and felt that the beginning of the walk was over. Hiking in the woods was now becoming the norm. It was what I did and expected to do every day. A tent was a familiar bedroom. This hotel room was not. I didn't like the generic corporate feel. There was no personality here, no individuality. I could be in any similar hotel anywhere in the world. I didn't want that. I wanted to be in Bonners Ferry and feel I was in Bonners Ferry.

A loud thunderstorm woke me early the next day. Watching the torrential rain and the lightning I thought maybe it was better I wasn't in the tent. Maybe. Necessary chores meant I needed to spend a day in town. But not at this hotel. I wanted somewhere more local and more in keeping with the town and, it must be admitted, less expensive. I found it at the Town and Country Motel, a much smaller local establishment at half the price. My main problem with Bonners Ferry was the same one I'd had in Eureka – the distance between the businesses I needed to patronise. The Post Office and library (where I wanted to use a computer to send reports back home – much easier than with the tiny

virtual keyboard on my phone) lay in the old town. The supermarket, laundromat and my new home lay on the highway two miles /3.2 kilometres away. I spent the day dashing up and down the main road, unable to organise a day in town properly. My head just wouldn't adjust to not being in the woods. The hurry was made worse by it being a Friday. The post office would be shut the next two days so I had to collect my box, change my clothes, wash the trail clothes in the laundromat, change my clothes back again, buy supplies, put any surplus in my box along with spare maps and books I'd read and then rush back to the post office to mail it. I made it with minutes to spare; hot, sweaty and breathless and with aching arms from carrying the box. I really didn't want to spend two more days in town though. Not that I had anything against Bonners Ferry. It was pleasant enough and had everything I needed but it was only a week since my last town stop and I didn't feel like resting. The next stage would take me ten days though so a stop here made sense. Carrying seventeen days supplies from Eureka would not have been a good idea.

The two establishments I liked most were the Badger's Den Café, where I had an excellent breakfast, and Bonners Books, where the proprietor recommended Rick Bass's *Winter* and I also bought a signed copy of *Sources of the River* by Jack Nisbet, which told the story of explorer and map maker David Thompson, the first person to chart the entire length of the Columbia River, whose catchment area I was in for most of the walk, all the way from the Continental Divide to the North Cascades. Thompson had arrived here in 1808 long before there was a ferry let alone a town and had traded with the local Kootenai tribe. These books would be my reading for the next week or so. Not wanting to use up any of my precious books I didn't open them in town, spending my second evening eating snacks, sorting gear and watching bad science fiction on the television.

Bonners Ferry information sign

CHAPTER 3

ROUGH COUNTRY

THE SELKIRK MOUNTAINS, BONNERS FERRY TO NORTHPORT

August 6 – 16

152 miles/245 km

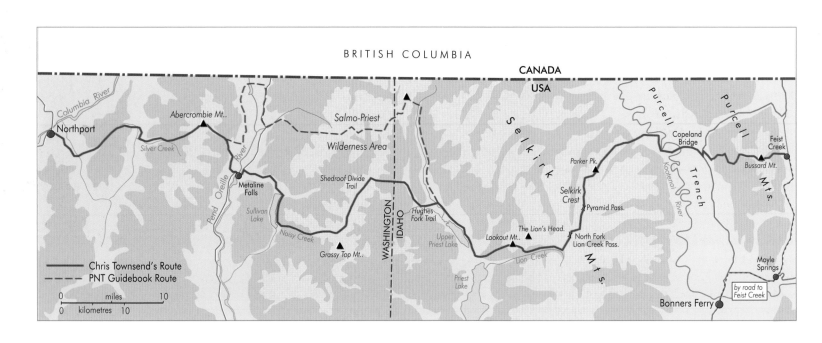

BRITISH COLUMBIA

CANADA

USA

Columbia River

Northport

Abercrombie Mt..

Silver Creek

Salmo-Priest

Wilderness Area

Pend Oreille River

Metaline Falls

Shedroof Divide Trail

Sullivan Lake

Noisy Creek

Grassy Top Mt..

WASHINGTON

IDAHO

Hughes Fork Trail

Upper Priest Lake

Lookout Mt..

The Lion's Head.

Priest Lake

Lion Creek

North Fork Lion Creek Pass.

Selkirk

Parker Pk.

Selkirk Crest

Pyramid Pass.

Mts.

Kootenai River

Purcell

Purcell

Trench

Mts.

Copeland Bridge

Feist Creek

Bussard Mt.

Moyle Springs

by road to Feist Creek

Bonners Ferry

—— Chris Townsend's Route
- - - PNT Guidebook Route

0   miles   10
0 kilometres 10

Twenty-four hours after leaving Bonners Ferry I woke to the sound of rain. I'd slept without a break for ten hours on a bumpy site with barely room for the tent, a far better sleep than I'd had in either room in Bonners Ferry. In the quiet, cool and dark of the woods was where my body and mind expected to be. Towns were too full of strange noises and the rooms were too warm for me to be comfortable. I'd left Bonners Ferry the morning before with Mike Ziegwied of North Country Transportation who drove me back to Feist Creek. Mike said he rarely came this way and he enjoyed driving through the woods. Meeting a hiker from Britain he found interesting too, telling me that he'd worked in London for a homeless charity many years ago. He'd had this company for the last eight years. Charging me a paltry $20 for the journey Mike said it had been an enjoyable change from his usual journeys to the airport and around the towns to the south. Before returning to the walk I popped into the restaurant for a last snack of soup and coffee and to thank them for their help. No charge, they said. I thanked them again. Long distance hikers call people like Mike and the restaurant staff 'trail angels' for the help they provide. On well-established and popular trails like the Appalachian and the Pacific Crest there are regular trail angels always available to provide assistance, often going out of their way to do so. The Pacific Northwest Trail is nowhere near that popular, with only a handful of hikers attempting the whole route every year, and there are few trail angels ready and waiting. Most, like Mike and the Feist Creek people, don't know in advance that hikers are likely to appear. Indeed, none of them knew about the PNT.

From the Moyie River valley I had one more forested ridge to cross before I would leave the Purcell Mountains behind and enter the Selkirk Mountains, a range that reputedly gave the toughest hiking and hardest navigation of the whole route as well as being splendidly wild and scenic. I was looking forward to the challenge and the landscape. First, though, I had to cross Bussard Mountain to the wide Purcell Trench and the Kootenai River, which separates the Purcells from the Selkirks. The long steep climb out of the Moyie River valley was less sweaty than other ascents as the day was cool and cloudy with only occasional brief bursts of sunshine. The route was a mix of old trails and forest roads. This looked a fairly heavily logged area and the forest was broken by regenerating clear-cuts, which did allow for some views of the hazy silhouettes of distant hills. Just one incident made the day stand out. I

Bear notice, Bussard Mountain

was sitting on a bank amongst tall plants having a snack and checking my maps when I heard a noise. Looking down the track I saw a black bear, another

cinnamon-coloured one, about a hundred yards away, watching me. I looked back for a while then stood up and started to noisily pack up. The bear stayed put. Then my maps rustled as I put them back in their plastic bag and the bear turned and ran down the track. The few moments when we had been staring at each other were wonderful and

I was able to admire the bear's beautiful coat and intelligent eyes. I suspect the vegetation around me blurred my outline and it wasn't sure what I was. The sound of paper rustling was obviously strange enough to make it decide running away was a good idea. Watching it bound down the track I realised again why running from a bear wasn't a good idea.

It was fast.

The cool day was welcome as there was no water on the day's walk. The guidebook mentioned some near the start of the descent after the traverse of Bussard Mountain but I found none, and neither had Li Brannfors the year before as beside the word 'spring' on the map he'd written 'no water'. Much further down the mountainside I came on Rock Creek, which is barely a trickle. It was enough though and I camped nearby. I'd only walked eleven miles/18 kilometres but it was enough as my pack was heavy with ten days food. Rain began just as my supper was ready. It was still raining the next morning. From the dampness all around it looked as though it had kept up all night. For once I had a hot breakfast, a packet of instant oatmeal that had lurked in the bottom of my food bag since Polebridge, and I set up the stove just outside the tent to heat water for it so I could stay in the tent.

'The Selkirks had better be impressive' was my thought after another tedious road walking day. Forest roads led down from Rock Creek to the highways and fields of the Purcell Trench where there were farms and wheat fields and the big Kootenai River, which is crossed via the Copeland Bridge. In the guidebook Ron writes 'the Copeland

The Kootenai River

Bridge is famous in PNTA history as the site of the first PNT sign. Pointing grandly east to the Continental Divide and west to the Pacific Ocean, it was erected by PNT volunteers in 1977 (and stolen by evil-doers in 1983)'. It has never been replaced and I still hadn't seen any mention of the PNT anywhere.

The hills were in cloud much of the day and light showers drifted down from the grey sky. The crossing of the valley was seven miles/11 kilometres long and I was relieved to reach the trailhead for the Parker Ridge Trail. Here I filled all my water containers – a heavy 5.7 litres – as a note from Li on my maps said he'd found no water for the next sixteen miles/26 kilometres. The guidebook and the map both showed a camp site near the trailhead. I couldn't find it and set off up the steep climb hoping to find a flat area and excited to be finally on a trail again. I was in luck. Not far above the valley floor some rocky knolls lined the trail. I clambered up to one and found it flat-topped and moss-covered. Pitching the tent was awkward as there was little soil for the pegs and I had to extend some guylines to the nearest logs and trees, but it was quite a scenic site and out of sight of any roads. I was now in the Selkirk Mountains.

Like the Purcells, the Selkirk Mountains are

Pyramid Lake

a long south-north trending range, most of which lies in Canada. Bounded by the Kootenai River on the east and the Columbia River to the north and west it's a distinct range that stretches across the Idaho panhandle, that narrow strip of Idaho running up to the Canadian border, and into northeast Washington State. The Selkirk Mountains are built of metamorphic rock with large intrusions of granite that forms steep rugged peaks and the fine rocky ridge of the Selkirk Crest, which I would traverse. There is one designated wilderness areas in the Selkirks, which I would cross, but again like the Purcells much of the area has suffered from clear-cut logging and is riddled with forest

Selkirk Crest scenery, Selkirk Mountains

country. Thankfully the morning clouds cleared and the afternoon was the sunniest for several days with the mountains sharp and clear. Prominent in the view was the Lion's Head, with its distinctive four summits. The wonderful scenery and the fine timberline walking continued along the ridge, skirting the summit of Long Mountain, to Pyramid Pass with Pyramid Peak rising above it. Having seen no hikers since Glacier I was a little startled to see a heavily laden backpacker approaching. Just out for a few days, he was heading for a camp at Long Mountain Lake, which lay in a bowl below the ridge. Not long afterwards another hiker approached who was also planning on camping at Long Mountain Lake. This second hiker was out of breath and told me he was out of shape. He was happy to stop for a chat and a rest. The first hiker had been moving fast and only paused briefly to speak to me. Both were wearing hiking boots and carrying big traditional packs that looked heavy. But then weight is less important when you're only out for a few days. Seeing my first other hikers didn't surprise me too much. I'd choose to come here before any of the other areas I'd crossed since Glacier.

Although the terrain was rough the navigation was easy. Just follow the ridge. There

roads, old and new. It's still wild but it's a battered wildness that's in need of restoration.

'Some of northern Idaho's finest back-packing', said Ron in the guidebook of the Parker Peak Trail along the Selkirk Crest to Pyramid Lake and Ball Lakes. It's certainly one of the best days on the whole PNT. The route follows a long curving ridge, forested at first, and then in open country. The initial climb up a myriad switchbacks is gentle but long and gives some views back down to the Purcell Trench. The world changes as the trail runs across a big rocky cirque below Parker Peak. Huge angled granite slabs rise into the sky and all around are rugged rocky peaks. This is real mountain

was a clear trail too. From Pyramid Pass it left the ridge and descended into a lovely cirque containing Pyramid Lake, where I planned camping, and which was situated under some big cliffs, an impressive place. Unsurprisingly there were many heavily used sites beside the lake with, as I was to discover, animals to go with them. After a long day it was almost dark when I camped and after eating I snuggled under my quilt and started falling asleep. Not much later loud rustling woke me. I peered out but my headlamp revealed nothing. I dozed off again. More rustling. More dozing. Then louder rustling and pans rattling. I started to think about bears and again scanned the site with my headlamp. A tiny mouse, all of an inch and a half long, scurried away. I hated to think how much noise a bear would make. At midnight I gave up and hung my food and pans from a high branch and brought my pack into the tent.

6 a.m. and I was woken by very noisy Stellar's jays screaming and chattering in the trees. These bright blue crested birds are beautiful to look at but horrible to hear; especially before dawn. A different noise alerted me to a more annoying nuisance – the steady whine of mosquitoes. Waterless forest camps might be less scenic but they were also quieter and bug free. I needed an early start anyway as much of the day would be cross-country in difficult terrain. I was on a trail for less than two miles/3 kilometres before it ran out at the two Ball Lakes. Now I had to find a way back up to the Selkirk Crest. The terrain was steep and rough; a complex mix of big rock slabs, boulders, precipitous grass, small whitebark pines and scree. A slow rising traverse with constant wandering about to find the best line with regard to both ease of passage and security led to the ridge. Aware that a slip could result in a long fall my concentration had been on the ground immediately in front of me. The world was confined to the rocks and grass and I felt close to the earth. The intricate details of

Selkirk Crest scenery, Selkirk Mountains

the patterns in the rocks (the markings of ancient earth movements), and the delicate traceries of the mountain plants filled my vision. Then as I reached the crest the landscape opened up and I could stand tall and look at the mountains. The world was suddenly vast, the complexity of the spreading mountain terrain echoing that of the miniature world of the slopes I had just climbed. The ridge itself was delightful, quite wide and with many little knobs and small wind shaped trees. Much of the time I walked on flat glacier-polished granite slabs. There was no trail and no need of one. The guidebook said 'you will be thankful for Vibram boot soles. This is not a place for missteps.' I didn't have Vibram boot soles. I didn't have boots. My trail shoes were fine. Ron was right though. High above the world on the remote crest of the Selkirk Mountains was not a place to slip.

The day changed when I left the ridge for a thousand foot/300 metre descent to North Fork Lion Creek Pass. A cairn marked the place where the route started down into the forest and for a few yards there was a bit of a trail. That soon vanished though and then it was tough bushwhacking, a desperate thrash through dense tall menziesia shrubs, whose pretty white flowers I'd been seeing for days, with hidden boulders and

Selkirk Crest scenery, Selkirk Mountains

fallen trees for entertainment. A compass bearing kept me on the right line to the broad pass where the undergrowth eased back and I could walk rather than stagger between the trees. Here I had a route choice. Li's map showed an alternative route along the Lion's Head ridge. The guidebook route was to continue down. The high level route looked by far the more interesting but as big clouds were building up I decided I didn't want to be up there in a thunderstorm so down the North Fork Lion Creek valley I went. The terrain was much less steep than on the descent to the pass but it was still overgrown with many obstacles and progress was slow. Traces of an old trail appeared occasionally

but frustratingly never lasted long. Throughout the descent I saw much bear scat and, where the ground was bare and soft, the huge hoof prints of moose. The creek, which I used as a guide so I didn't stray too far from the route, was a lovely stream, cascading over water-smoothed granite slabs. Near the bottom of the valley a massive bull moose suddenly appeared out of the trees and crossed the trail. I managed to grab one poor photo of it disappearing back into the trees. I'd forgotten just how big these largest members of the deer family are. Seeing this prehistoric-looking monster deer was the highlight of the descent.

The North Fork Lion Creek led to Lion Creek itself and more bushwhacking until I reached the Lion Creek Trail, a closed forest road that felt like a city pavement. Suddenly I could walk normally and at a reasonable speed. Soon I reached the trailhead and was on a dirt road, with occasional vehicles and some roadside camps. From one clearing loud rock music blared out. I left the road for the next ascent, which led to Lookout Mountain, though I wasn't intending going very far before I camped, just out of sight and sound of the road. Again the trail was a closed forest road that was slowly becoming overgrown. I found a stony site on the edge of this track with a view across the Lion Creek

valley to huge smooth, glacier-carved granite slabs. I was relieved to stop. It had been a long, arduous day. I'd only walked ten miles/16 kilometres but it had taken me ten and a half hours. I'd crossed the High Selkirks though, and it had been glorious.

Having spent a day mostly descending, all the way down to 1400 feet/425 metres, I now had to climb all the way back up to 6767 foot/2063 metre Lookout Mountain. If I'd taken Li's route over the Lion's Head I'd have stayed high and not had to deal with the bushwhacking or a long arduous ascent. But on a long distance walk decisions once made are usually final. Going back is not an option. I had another choice here in fact. I didn't actually have to climb Lookout Mountain. I could have simply walked down the road in the Lion Creek valley to the where the trail joined it on the western side of the mountain. That would have been dull and boring though and only an option I'd have considered if the weather had been really foul. Long distance hiking isn't about the physically easiest or the quickest route but rather about the most wild, exciting and satisfying, which can also mean the most arduous and challenging. As it was, the sky was cloudy but it was also dry and calm so up the mountain I went.

The ascent was mostly in forest, with some

views of big Priest Lake far below. I was on the summit of Lookout Mountain in two and a half hours. Although the sky was grey the clouds were above the summits and the mountains looked tremendous. Along the snaking crest I could see the distinctive blocky tops of the Lion's Head. Out of the Lion Creek valley rose great sloping walls of polished granite. Appropriately a tall lookout tower rose from the summit. I heard voices and noticed men on the tower, a work crew doing repairs. One of the workers came down for a chat and told me about his love of the area and how he particularly enjoyed backcountry skiing here. As a keen ski tourer I could see that skiing here would be exciting and challenging. The terrain was steep. On open slopes there could be much avalanche danger. Finding routes through the forest could be difficult too. But winter here would be thrilling and intense with the scars of summer, the logged areas and dirt roads, covered by deep snow and the mountains shining and frozen.

Soon after starting the descent I was surprised to meet groups of walkers heading up, eleven people in all. They didn't look like hikers who'd come far and were dressed more in casual urban clothing than mountain gear. I soon realised why as I came on a roadhead with a large car park

Camp on lower slopes of Lookout Mountain above Lion Creek, Selkirk Mountains

only a short walk from the summit. This wasn't marked on my maps. My route quickly disappeared back into the trees as it continued down the long south-west ridge of the mountain on old trails with many blow-downs and some sketchy sections. Above me the clouds cleared and the sun shone but I was soon in magnificent western red cedar forest where it was dark and cool. In the shadows grew strange ghostly saprophytic plants, which can't obtain energy through photosynthesis and so have no green colouring or need of sunlight but instead are parasites, feeding on fungi in the soil that in turn live off tree roots. I identified one cluster of weird almost translucent white flowers as Indian pipes and some tall reddish ones as spotted coralroot. These plants spoke of an alien sunless world that felt cold and shivery.

The trail became harder and harder to find as it entered a heavily logged area, frequently disappearing amongst logging debris, dense undergrowth and tightly packed new trees. An option was to abandon it and take a forest road down the last section to the Priest valley. After losing the trail one last time in some thickets of new growth I gave up and took the easy route. The passage through the logged forest didn't seem to offer any rewards that would have made the difficult bushwhacking worthwhile. Li had written on the map 'good luck in trying to find red line in here' (the 'official' PNT route was marked on the map in red). I didn't have that luck. Even using the roads was confusing as I made guesses at each junction as to which branch to take. I was looking for the Floss Creek Trail, which would take me to Upper Priest Lake. A sign appeared on the disused logging road I was following. This was the Floss Creek Trail. I'd found it without realising it. I checked my position with the GPS and was pleased to see I'd come farther than I'd thought. Whilst the GPS was useful for pinpointing my position it was useless for help with the route when I was

View along the Selkirk Crest from Lookout Mountain, Selkirk Mountains

following roads or trails not marked on the map as it couldn't tell me where they went. Now I knew I was on the right trail I could stride out without worrying whether it would take me in the wrong direction. The road walk did give one reward when a bull moose, smaller and more spindly than the one I'd seen the previous day, loped across in front of me.

The trail soon reached Upper Priest Lake, a serene body of water set amidst densely wooded hills. Unlike the small mountain lakes, which at home would be called lochans (little lakes), this was a real lake, being over 2 miles/3 kilometres long and half a mile/one kilometre wide. It forms the heart of the Upper Priest Lake Scenic Area. It was dusk as I walked beside the lake and the trees were casting deep shadows on the blue water. Gentle ripples ruffled the surface occasionally but I could feel no wind. This was a quiet subtle beauty, soft and calming and totally unlike the stark, exciting and challenging beauty of the mountains. I camped at Trapper Creek Campground which had picnic tables, fire pits, bear boxes (bear proof metal containers) for food storage and cleared tent sites, making it the most organised backcountry site I'd used since Glacier National Park. Someone was here for a long stay as one of the sites was strewn with masses of

Indian Pipes

gear – ice boxes, double burner stove, tent, tarp, external frame pack. There was no-one home but just after dark I heard a gentle swishing sound on the water and saw the silhouette of a figure in a canoe pulling into the bank.

During the evening I heard some distant shouting and the roar of motor boats then all was

quiet until a deer in camp woke me at 5.45 a.m. The sky was pink. I leapt up and went down to the lake to watch the beautiful soft dawn. Moving my kitchen into an old fire ring on a gravel beach I watched the clouds turn a soft red, their dappled patterns reflected in the almost motionless water.

The magical dawn world fading into more

mundane day I packed up and set off along the trail which followed the lake and then the Upper Priest valley through a majestic forest of giant cedars and hemlocks. I came out of the trees onto a road by a large Forest Service notice board for the Upper Priest Lake Trail. Amongst the neatly printed waterproof signs was a rather scruffy paper one encased in a plastic bag. The top half was a black and white map with 'PNT Alternate' hand written on it with a felt tip pen. After nearly 300 miles/480 kilometres I'd finally found a mention of the PNT. A printed notice underneath the map headed in red 'Attention Pacific Northwest Thru Hikers' said that the guidebook route to the north of here was not recommended due to severe erosion and fire damage and recommended a 5 mile/8 kilometre diversion on forest roads to the Hughes Fork Trail, which would lead back to the PNT. The Hughes Fork Trail was also marked as a suggested route on Li's maps, along with a connecting trail that cut out half the road walking but did involved '1 mile of alder-choked frustration'. With the previous days' bushwhacking all too fresh in my mind and on my arms and legs, which were covered in tiny scratches and weals, I decided a longer road walk was preferable and set off on the Forest Service diversion.

Having plodded round the roads I was heading for the Hughes Fork Trail when I came on a junction with another trail, the Jackson Creek Trail, which, I saw from the maps, would lead up to an alternative route Li had marked on the map. Being already south of the guidebook route I decided to join this route and headed up the Jackson Creek Trail. Part way up I left Idaho for the third and last state on the PNT, Washington. At the state line I also entered the Salmo-Priest Wilderness Area, the first designated wilderness area on the walk. This 41,335 acre wilderness forms a curious u-shape in the western Selkirk Mountains, taking in two long mountain ridges but not the wide valley between them. There are magnificent Douglas fir and western hemlock forests in the wilderness and it is home to much wildlife.

With no information on the Jackson Creek Trail I hoped it wouldn't be too difficult to follow, especially in the dense forest of the lower slopes. In fact although there were some brushy sections, a few blowdowns and occasional muddy sections the trail was mostly straightforward. As I climbed the sky darkened and rain began to fall, steadily and persistently. The big trees shielded me from most of it and my broad-brimmed hat kept the rest of it off so I didn't bother with waterproof clothing.

Although the maps showed the trail climbing away from the creek to reach the crest not far from a spring, by which I had intended to camp, the trail in fact followed the creek all the way to the ridge. This was a mile/1.2 kilometres from the spring. However there was water here and enough space for my tent in the narrow defile at the head of the valley so I made camp. Light rain was still falling and the air was damp and cool. Once I stopped I soon cooled down and felt chilly in just a thin shirt and shorts. In situations like this it's important to warm up as soon as possible. The colder you become, the harder it is to restore body heat and the longer it takes, with the risk of hypothermia always present. This was one reason I was carrying spare dry clothing. I quickly stripped off my damp shirt and shorts – keeping them on under dry layers would have kept me feeling chilly until they dried – and then donned my wool t-shirt, fleece sweater, windshirt, long pants, dry wool socks and wool hat and had the pleasure of feeling the warmth returning. I set up my kitchen under a big spruce tree, to which was attached a Jackson Creek Trail sign. The needle-covered ground under the tree was dry so I reckoned it would keep off the rain, as it proved when there was a heavy shower. The ground around my camp was lush with flowers, grasses and

Dawn at Upper Priest Lake, Selkirk Mountains

bushes. I felt in an enclosed world that could have been oppressive but in fact felt protective.

At dawn there was still a damp chill in the air but sunlight was filtering through the trees and high above I could see blue sky. The day was one of a succession of good trails, all named – Shedroof Divide, Grassy Top, Grassy-Hall Divide, Noisy Creek, Lakeshore – that linked nicely together and took me down from the Wilderness Area to big Sullivan Lake. With no route finding, no big ascents and feeling strong after over three weeks of hiking the walking felt effortless and I was surprised in the evening to discover I'd covered 22 miles/35 kilometres.

Mostly I was in forest but from high on the ridge in the morning there were good views from beautiful open meadows and not so attractive burned areas back to the ragged line of the Selkirk Crest and over line after line of rounded wooded hills. The latter had a patchwork quilt look, created by the big squares of clear-cuts, some fresh, some regenerating. The Wilderness Area felt like an island, a tiny sliver of untouched forest high above the damaged lands. There was little sign of wildlife in the forest other than many grouse with chicks, which ran away in front of me along the trails.

A big busy campground lay at the southern end of Sullivan Lake. I passed by and found a quiet spot half way along the roadless eastern shore. There were no mosquitoes, the sky was clear and it was quite warm down here at 2600 feet/800 metres so for the first time on the walk I slept out without the tent, lying under a big Douglas fir and looking up through its branches to the stars. I was soon disturbed by a small animal gnawing on my gear, a ground squirrel from the brief glimpse I had of it. Even when I moved my food next to my head it came back so I ended up bundling everything into the pack and hanging it from a spike on a tree. I could also hear cars and voices from the road on the far side of the lake but these soon faded and my sleep was then undisturbed.

The next night, far from sleeping under the stars in the woods, I was in a room in a hotel, the Washington Hotel in Metaline Falls. This was an old-fashioned hotel – no TV, no radio, no telephone, no air conditioning, no ensuite facilities. Just a room with a bed and some bits of furniture. The cost was only $40 and that included laundry. Unsurprisingly there was no internet connection or Wi-Fi in the hotel, or anywhere in the town for that matter, so I would have to wait a few days before I could send emails and contact the outside world. Still, no one was expecting to hear from me yet as Metaline

Falls was not one of my planned town stops.

After walking the short trail to the end of Sullivan Lake I had been on hot, dusty, paved roads for the eight miles/13 kilometres into the town. These roads were quiet until the last curving main highway, which was a frightening combination of blind bends, narrow shoulders and fast vehicles. I reckoned this was the most dangerous part of the walk so far and I was relieved to reach the town centre.

I hadn't originally planned on coming through Metaline Falls as the guidebook route passes some six miles/10 kilometres away and it was only a couple more days to Northport, which lay on the trail. However Li's alternative route that I'd adopted came through the town so here I was. Wandering round the town I was glad I'd come this way. Metaline Falls was small and pleasant with a slightly decayed air. It was situated on the Pend Oreille River, a tributary of the Columbia, which I'd been reading about in *Sources of the River*. Travelling down the Pend Oreille David Thompson had been stopped here in 1809 by the Metaline Falls, today under the waters of a reservoir. The town was founded in 1900 to serve nearby zinc-lead mines. The short main street offered a post office, gift shops, Cathy's café, Heidi's bar

restaurant and a small supermarket. There was also a visitor centre in an old railway carriage that had some information about the town but mostly just shelves of second-hand books. Amongst these I found a copy of Mary Stewart's *The Crystal Cave*, about Merlin and the Arthurian legends. I'd been interested in these stories since childhood and had read this novel many years before. Now I would read it again, far from the Celtic lands that gave rise to the myths.

I had lunch in Cathy's, topped up my supplies in the supermarket (just adequate for hikers), and had dinner and beer in Heidi's. In the last I was told that around ten PNT hikers had been through before me this year, mostly in groups of two or three, and including Nimblewill Nomad, who was with a companion and had van support. He was a week ahead of me now so it seemed unlikely I would meet him. I liked Metaline Falls – it was nice and compact with friendly people, distinctive old buildings and a fine backdrop of crags and forest.

Back in the hotel I checked through my gear. My pack was causing problems with the shoulder straps twisting and the foam padding ,in them deforming. On examination it also had a surprising number of tears and holes, more than I'd realised. Aside from becoming less comfortable

Dusk and moon on the descent of Abercrombie Mountain, Selkirk Mountains

I now doubted it would last the trip. I would have to contact the makers, GoLite, and hope they could send me a replacement. I was puzzled as this was a new pack, although a model I had used extensively in the past without any problems. Maybe, I thought, I had a rogue pack that had slipped through quality control. It happens. My camera was playing up too, the autofocus, which was built into the lens, working intermittently. I really didn't want to have to somehow replace that as well. To add to all this my feet ached from the pavement pounding. Feeling frustrated. I eased the tension by complaining in my journal. 'Things! Packs, cameras, feet. Bugger!'

The altitude of Metaline Falls is 2100 feet/640 metres. From the town my route led over Abercrombie Mountain, some 12 miles/19 kilometres away by trail, which is 7308 feet/2227 metres high. The day out of Metaline Falls was going to be tough. To fortify myself I had a large and excellent omelette breakfast in Cathy's Café, a nice change from my usual muesli. Eggs are one of the foods I miss on the trail. Powdered versions just don't taste right to me and whilst there are protective containers for the real thing, and you can break them into plastic bottles, the weight and risk of a messy spillage puts me off carrying them. By not doing so I could relish them even more in towns.

Abercrombie Mountain (the unusual name comes from Lieutenant W.A. Abercrombie, who travelled the Pend Oreille River in 1879 and 1883) is the high point on the westernmost ridge of the Selkirk Mountains. It would also be the high point of my walk so far. First though I had to climb the steep slopes west of Metaline Falls. Li marked two routes on his map, a 2 mile/3.2 kilometre loop on a road or a ¼ mile/0.4 kilometre steep climb up a game trail. I opted for the latter, a very steep 400 foot/122 metre clamber through bushes and forest, that had me sweaty and panting. I recovered on the long gently graded forest road walk that followed, during which I read most of the time. This led to the Flume Creek Trail and the ascent of the massive eastern shoulder of Abercrombie Mountain. Coming out of the trees I walked up the loose talus that makes up the fine rocky summit cone. The flattened remnants of an old lookout tower lay nearby. Abercrombie is far higher than any nearby peaks other than Hooknose Mountain just to the north-east and so gives extensive views all around, including to distant mountains on which snow fields were visible. Again I was struck by the patchwork appearance created by the extensive logging that had taken place on nearby hills.

A late start, the long ascent and an hour on the summit meant that it was almost dusk when I started down on the North Fork Silver Creek Trail. The descent was on long gentle switchbacks through big trees (Ron describes these as 'frustratingly easy' in the guidebook). I was kept entertained by a dark red sunset and an almost half-full waxing moon, soon followed by one bright star shining low against the sunset – actually the planet Venus I guessed. As I descended the trees grew bigger and the forest floor darker. I prefer to hike at night without a light as I feel more in touch with my surroundings and my night sight is quite good. Eventually though, after stumbling over yet another invisible root, I switched on my headlamp and finished the descent locked into its cone of artificial light. If I'd found any water I'd have camped but there was none until I reached the valley floor and the big Silver Creek campground with hitching posts, fire rings and an outhouse. The site looked well-used so, remembering the rodent problems at other camps, I hung my food from a high branch and took my pack into the tent with me. Under a tree I found a pair of high-topped leather Red Wing boots with stacked heels and Vibram soles. A pair of socks was tucked into them. Nearby was a flat stone and I guessed that the owner had sat on this while changing their footwear after going out horse riding and had then forgotten their boots. This could only have been a day or so ago as the boots were dry and in good condition.

The Selkirk Mountains were behind me now and there was just a hot day's road walking to Northport on the Columbia River. At first it was dirt roads in the forest, from one of which a coyote watched me carefully before trotting away, but soon I was on paved roads in a mix of farmland and woodland. Footsore and bored I was glad to reach Northport where I headed for the Matteson House B&B, which Li had recommended and had said he'd

Remnants of a log cabin, Purcell Mountains

let them know I was coming. Even so I was surprised when the front door opened and a friendly-looking woman said 'you must be Chris, come in, dinner's on the table'. Feeling a little overwhelmed I was soon sitting at a large table with other guests and Bertha – 'Bert' – and Jerry Matteson enjoying an excellent home-cooked meal. Li had written 'PNT friendly' on the map. That's an understatement. The Mattesons went out of their way to be helpful, doing my laundry and providing three meals a day, all at a very low cost. I was very pleased to have planned a day off here. I couldn't have found anywhere better.

Little Northport – population about 300 –

was a delightful town too. It was also compact, something that after the long walks in Eureka and Bonners Ferry, I was very pleased about, with every facility I needed just a short walk from the Mattesons. Nestled on an area of flat ground between Silver Crown Mountain and the Columbia River (here trapped in the Franklin D. Roosevelt Lake, a reservoir) Northport didn't have much space in which to spread out. It began life in the 1880s as a port for steamer services on the Columbia River but soon became a railway town and the northernmost stop on the Spokane Falls and Northern Railway, hence the name. My day in the town was spent on the usual chores. I emailed GoLite about my now frankly uncomfortable pack and had a quick reply from company founder Coup Couponas, a good friend of mine whom I'd met several times and once been backpacking with in the Uinta Mountains in Utah. I hated having to tell him the pack had failed. He generously offered to send me a new pack to the next town on my walk, Oroville. Now I just had to get this one the 200 miles/322 kilometres there without it falling apart.

I reckoned it would take me ten days to reach Oroville. Northport's small supermarket had just enough suitable food though no muesli or granola for breakfast so I bought instant oatmeal

instead. Still, at least the latter was easily portable, unlike the only cereal on offer in a small town in the Pyrenees on a walk there long ago. Corn flakes are too fragile for carrying and don't offer much energy either. On that walk I settled for bread and cheese for breakfast. This time I would supplement the oatmeal with dried fruit.

My evenings at the Mattesons were spent in pleasant conversations with them and their guests, some of whom were working in the area. None were long distance walkers and they were curious as to why I was doing this. I tried to explain about the joy of simply walking every day, of feeling in touch with nature, of revelling in wild places and wild life, of the pleasure of feeling my pace fitted in with the landscape. I don't know how much of this I truly conveyed but talking about it did bring some realisation as to how I was progressing. I was now well into the walk. The worries that always emerge early on – would I find the route, a campsite, water; did I have enough time; could I actually do this – had long gone. I felt at home with the walk now. It was what I did and I was confident doing it. Not having those concerns meant I could go deeper into the real reasons for spending a summer walking in the wilds and that was to enjoy being there. As Hamish Brown put it in *Hamish's*

Mountain Walk, the story of the first walk over all Scotland's Munros (3,000 foot mountains) and a book that inspired me as a novice long distance hiker and still does, 'life should be lived greatly from day to day'. I know of no better way of doing that than on a long distance walk.

The Matteson's B&B, Northport

CHAPTER 4

THE KETTLE CREST

NORTHPORT TO OROVILLE

August 18 – 27

205 miles/330 km

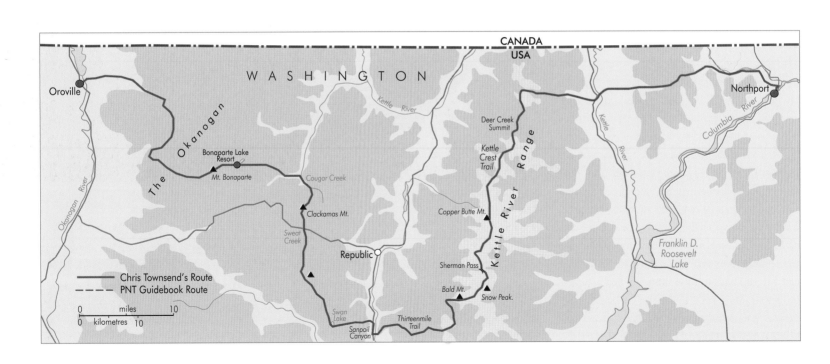

I tried to remember my positive feelings about long distance walking during the first two days out of Northport. They were, frankly, not enjoyable and in some respects quite depressing as I went through some of the most abused and little-cared for terrain on the whole walk. The Mattesons had encouraged me to stay a second day but after one day in town I wanted to be walking again. A few hours after setting off I wasn't so sure; or rather, I wasn't so sure I wanted to be walking here. I could have been in the Selkirks or Glacier National Park or many other scenic landscapes. Why was I spending time walking through country that made me feel fed up? The answer was that this was an inevitable part of a long distance walk. There are always connecting sections between the wildest and most enjoyable areas that are less interesting, dull or, as in this case, so damaged as to be disillusioning. However, to skip these sections and break the walk up would be to lose the continuity of the journey and the continuity of seeing the landscape unfold and watching how it changed and how the different natural areas merged into each other. Slowly I was building up a big picture of the environs of the PNT. The rhythm of the walk, which was now part of my life, was important too and would cease if I didn't walk the whole way. The

The Kettle River

key though was balance. There had to be enough inspiration and joy to outweigh the uninspiring and deflating sections.

The way out of town was across a big highway bridge over the Columbia River, the northernmost such bridge in the USA. Jerry said walking across the bridge was too dangerous and insisted on driving me across. I didn't feel I could refuse him but after he'd gone I walked back across the bridge into Northport to maintain the continuity of the route. There was a space between the guard rail for the road and the outer rail anyway so I was separated from the traffic. There would be far more dangerous road walks to come. The rest of the day was spent

on gravel and dirt roads through heavily managed second and third growth forest with some ugly clear-cuts and large piles of logging detritus. There was also much roadside litter, especially empty beer cans; far more than I had seen anywhere else. I felt this was a despised and trashed landscape and that the people who came here had no respect for it. The sun was blazing down from the sky and it was the hottest day since Polebridge. I passed a fire information sign that gave the fire risk as extreme. The mounds of logging debris and the dense new growth would burn all too easily I thought.

The area was also used for cattle grazing. There were hoof prints and cowpats everywhere and I saw two herds where the road crossed big meadows. For the first time on the walk I felt it unwise to drink straight from streams. Water would have to be boiled or treated with my UV light purifier. I camped just out of sight of the road near a small creek. It was not a memorable camp. The next day was worse – 'probably the most tedious of the walk so far' I wrote in my journal. Most of the very hot day was spent on a slow climb on gravel roads through more logged forest that was tiring for my feet, my shoulders and, especially, my mind. Initially I had walked through farmland and privately owned forest with keep out notices and barbed wire fences everywhere. I'd stopped where I had the previous night because I knew from the maps that this section was coming up. Once through this confined, restricted country I reached the Kettle River and the Rock Cut Bridge, beyond which the ascent began. I wrote down more negative thoughts – 'a real trudge. No feeling of contact with land. No views. Nasty clear-cuts'. I was not a happy walker. Then, just as I was thinking I needed to camp soon, the route left the road for an old closed to vehicles one that was reverting back to a trail. My journal tone changed -'instant contact with nature. Crunching on fir cones and needles not gravel. Trees hanging over trail. Brush.

Kettle Crest Trail sign

Reality.' Such a little change it might have seemed to an outsider yet to me it was vast. Happiness returned. After 3 miles/4.8 kilometres of this fading road I camped at a long abandoned road junction where an old signpost was still visible, a good forest site.

During the day I'd had glimpses of the forested hills of the Kettle River Range, where I would be for the next few days. The dry country of eastern Washington looks flat and uninteresting for walking on the map, as it had seemed when I came through it with Kris and Leanne en route to the start of the walk. Just dusty rolling plains under a hot sun. Look more closely at the map though and a strip of green runs across the top of the state, just south of the Canadian border, a strip broken only briefly by the Okanogan lowlands. This is where the PNT runs, through the little-known forests and mountains of north-east Washington. After two days and 40 miles/64 kilometres of unpleasant walking I hoped the Kettle Range, would live up to the guidebook claim that it was one of the highlights of the entire trail.

I was surprised the next morning to feel cold when I sat up and shrugged off my quilt. I looked at the thermometer, just 1.4°C/34.5°F, which made it the coldest night of the walk by far. I wore my

View from the Kettle Crest Trail, Kettle River Range

down jacket during breakfast. High above though the sky was clear and I could see sunshine on the tree tops. The day was mostly in forest but it was on trails and any clear-cuts were well overgrown so I felt more relaxed and less full of suppressed anger than on the last two days. Any views came in some big burned areas from where I could see the rolling green Kettle hills. I touched a road at a pass called Deer Creek Summit where a notice showed a network of groomed cross-country ski trails and said this was the Deer Creek Nordic Sno-Park. Across the road another sign announced the Kettle Crest National Recreation Trail, which I would follow for many miles. Although I was back

The Old Stage Trail crossing the Kettle Crest

up high again at around 6,000 feet/1830 metres there were signs of the more arid nature of this part of Washington with brown treeless slopes, dusty trails and meadows full of sagebrush.

I hadn't seen any more cows or signs of cows until late in the day when I was high on the Kettle Crest and then suddenly there were masses of them along with masses of dung. A series of springs lies along the crest. The first one I came to, Neff Spring, was fenced with the spring covered over and the water piped to a stock tank. The area all around was trampled into an unpleasant semi-liquid mix of mud and dung by the cattle. In case further springs were trashed I filled my water containers.

Sure enough, the very next one, Midnight Spring, was just a filthy trickle in a cattle polluted morass. Not far beyond this ruined spring I reached a saddle where an old stagecoach route, now the Old Stage Trail, crossed the crest. Situated between Midnight Mountain and Copper Butte this was a fine spot for a camp. Small trees dotted the saddle but just below was a huge burn with many dead trees still standing. Through the stark silhouettes of these I watched a deep crimson sunset over distant hills, an unusual scene. A cool westerly breeze sweeping over the saddle had me pitching the whole tent. On the last two nights just the mesh inner had done, and that was only needed in case of bugs.

The next day was one of the finest on the walk, fully justifying Ron's statement in the guidebook, starting with a subtle dawn with soft layers of cloud and a little yellow and pink colour. I enjoyed being at a site with spacious views and spent some time watching the landscape and taking photographs. By the time I was ready to leave the sun was shining, though the sky remained mostly hazy all day with high thin cloud and flat light. I followed the Kettle Crest Trail and grew to love it. It would remain one of my favourite trails of the whole walk. Initially the trail took me over 7149 foot/2179 metre Copper Butte and then

along the rollicking, rolling crest all the way to Bald Mountain, below which I camped. The trail skirted most summits but was never far from the ridgeline. The mountains were not dramatic rock peaks but more rounded wooded hills. However unlike many of the densely forested hills further east the forest was more open and they had many big meadows, mostly on south and west slopes, that gave them an airy unrestricted feel. There were still flowers in these meadows – pale violet lupins, pink and white asters and red paintbrush.

The trail crossed a road at Sherman Pass and as I approached it in quick succession I met two pairs of horse riders, four mountain bikers and a day hiker. Just across the pass I met another day hiker and a family of three collecting huckleberries. Thirteen people on the trail were the most I'd met in one day since Glacier National Park. Indeed, most days I'd seen no-one. It was a Saturday but there had been other Saturdays. I noticed in the trail register at the pass that 2 parties of 2 were camping overnight, en route for Snow Peak and Bald Mountain, so I wasn't surprised to see a scattering of tents near a spring by an old cabin on the slopes of Snow Peak. I'd passed a trail maintenance sign and a small digger before the spring and reckoned that three guys sitting on chairs outside three tents

were probably the work crew as they looked settled in. The other camps looked more like the temporary ones of overnight backpackers.

I carried on beneath Snow Peak towards Bald Mountain. Crossing the steep stony slopes of this peak I started to think about camping and then noticed some flat ground in a rocky bowl well below the trail. I dropped down to it and found a dramatic camp site, one of the best of the whole walk. Above me the scree and rock covered slopes, dotted with trees, rose towards the hidden summit of Bald Mountain. Below me dark green forest stretched into the distance. It was dusk when I made camp and soon dark. My real enjoyment of the site came the next day as the dawn light was beautiful with a blue sky and long tree shadows giving great depth to the wild landscape.

High thin clouds soon drifted in though, as they had on the previous day, and the day became hazier, as did my mind, my concentration being poor, which led to a couple of frustrating navigation errors. The first one was unbelievably stupid. I knew from the map that not much farther along the Kettle Crest Trail I should leave it for the Ebbs Mountain Trail yet I still walked right past the signed junction, only realising my mistake when I'd descended several hundred feet and was half a mile

away. Once I'd retraced my steps I found the Ebbs Mountain Trail was another scenic Kettle Range trail with more open meadows. It was faint in places and I had to look out for cairns, cut logs and plastic flagging to stay on route. The PNT eventually left the trail for a cross-country bushwhack down to an old road. Here I made my second, more understandable mistake, allowing easier terrain to push me too far west, which resulted in my hitting a different abandoned road. After a little while I managed to sort out where I was, find the right road and follow it to the Thirteenmile Trail, which ran through fine Alpine larch, Douglas fir and ponderosa pine forest. The last tree, an old favourite from walks in Arizona and southern California, was a sign of the aridity of this area. Also known as yellow pine ponderosa pine is an impressive tree with yellow-brown bark that forms thick plates and glows in the sun. Combined with the feathery-looking yellow-green bundles of long needles this gives ponderosa pine forests a light, airy feel compared with the darker, more sombre ambience of the spruces and firs found in damper and higher areas. At one point a long thin snake undulated across the trail in front of me. It was moving slowly and I was able to admire its fine markings and identify it as a western terrestrial garter snake, a non-poisonous species.

With a waterless section coming up the guidebook advised carrying water from near Jack Shelburg's cabin, which lay below the PNT, so I dropped down to it on the oddly named Bear Pot Trail, finding the cabin a gloomy ruin in a shadowy dense lodgepole pine forest. The nearby creek was barely flowing and the water was dark and dirty. I filled my containers anyway but headed back up to the trail in search of somewhere more cheerful to camp. As I climbed the next hill there was a shower of rain and a faint rainbow. Descending to the next creek I found it flowing more strongly than the one at the cabin. It was much cleaner too. There was nowhere flat to camp however so having emptied and refilled my containers I walked on to eventually camp on open ground in the woods below the trail.

This was the twenty-seventh camp on the walk. The routine of setting up a home in the woods (it almost always was in the woods) had become almost automatic. First I would find a suitable flat area, lying down on the ground if it was dry to check it was flat enough and if there was a slight slope so I could set up camp with my head uphill (if I sleep with my head downhill I wake with a headache). I would then decide which of four options looked best for shelter – none at all, just sleep out under the stars, which I only did a few times; just the mesh inner tent if biting insects might be a problem; outer tent on its own if rain or dew might be a problem and there was no or little wind; and inner and outer together if any combination of rain, bugs and wind were likely (wind because the inner tent lower walls kept it off my quilt). Even in fine weather I liked to sort my shelter out first as only then could I relax. This stems from my Scottish camping background. In the Highlands sites are usually on open hillsides with no trees for shelter and it's often raining and windy when making camp so pitching the tent and getting under cover is a priority. The weather can change fast in Scotland too so, even when it's fine,

The summit of Copper Butte, Kettle Crest

Dusk in a burnt forest, Kettle River Range

setting up the tent is a good idea. Only when my tent is up do I feel I can slow down. In Scotland camping often means living in the tent too, with all my gear undercover and the stove set up in the tent vestibule. One of the pleasures of this trip was the sheltered woodland sites where I could sit outside to cook, eat, read, write and look around, relegating the tent to just being a bedroom. With this in mind I had brought a small piece of closed cell foam that was waterproof and provided a little padding and insulation to put on wet ground or cold rocks and use as a seat (when sleeping it went under my feet). Ideally I would have a tree or a rock as a backrest too. The stove I would set up on bare ground or a flat stone so it couldn't scorch or set fire to vegetation, usually a good twenty feet or more from the tent. When the weather was unsettled, though, I brought the stove close to the tent overnight so if it was cold or rainy in the morning I could make a hot drink without leaving my shelter. Around my stove I would arrange my kitchen items – pots, spoons, knife, stove fuel, food, water containers. On the other side of my seat went maps and guidebook pages, notebook and pens, paperbacks, weather meter, smartphone, binoculars and headlamp. Thus I could sit back and relax with everything I might need during the evening to hand. Without moving I could make hot drinks, cook dinner, study maps and guidebook, make notes, read, check the barometer and watch wildlife. If dry my camera would be attached to the tripod and stood nearby so it was ready for low light photos at sunset and sunrise.

Making notes at a camp on the Kettle Crest Trail, Kettle River Range

For some long distance hikers camping is just a necessary chore. They may stop for a meal earlier in the day and then walk until dark or later, throw up their shelter, go straight to sleep and then move on at first light, perhaps before having any breakfast, which will be eaten later on the trail. I'm the opposite. I like camping, I like creating a temporary home in the wilds, so I like to have

enough time to enjoy my camps. If I make camp late, perhaps after dark, then if the camp is scenic I'll have a leisurely morning before leaving. If I find a lovely site I may stop early so I can camp there. In camp I can unwind and take in my surroundings, noticing the details and textures that are easily missed when hiking. I can watch wildlife, whether beetles or eagles, without feeling I ought to be moving on. If the weather is stormy just lying in my tent listening to the rain beating on the fabric whilst I am warm and dry is pleasurable too. Because sites were important to me I didn't want to be tied to water sources and so had two big collapsible containers in which I could carry ample water for a camp and into the next day's hiking. This was the third day in a row that I'd carried water the last few miles before camping.

As there had been several short showers during the day and there were big clouds in the sky at this camp I pitched both inner and outer and set up my kitchen close to the tent. The site was pleasant, set amidst big ponderosa pines and long grasses. I left the tent door open when I lay down to sleep, as I always did unless the weather prevented me. I didn't want to cut myself off from the outdoors anymore than necessary. At dawn the sound of squirrels chattering woke me up, a

pleasant natural alarm clock. The tent outer was wet with dew on the outside and condensation on the inside. The sky was clear and the pressure had risen rapidly so it looked as though the unsettled weather, which had only produced a little rain, was over. I had a double helping of oatmeal for breakfast for the second morning running. I was eating more during the day too. My appetite had increased, as it always did three to four weeks into a long walk. I would now eat considerably more on most days than I had so far yet I would still finish the walk noticeably lighter and thinner than at the start. This meant that even though I'd left Northport with a pack bulging with food intended to last ten days I was now likely to run short. There was the option of diverting to the little town of Republic, which lay some 8.5 miles/13.7 kilometres from the PNT, and which Li described as a 'cool town' but I didn't want to leave the route whether by hitch-hiking or a road walk. Instead I decided to rely on Bonaparte Lake Resort, which I would reach a couple of days before Oroville and which Li marked on the map as a 'possible resupply'. If there was nothing there, well, a couple of days on short rations wouldn't hurt me.

My last day in the Kettle River Range was another fine one. The Thirteenmile Trail continued

over the rolling brown and green hills, with many open meadows in the forest giving views over the Sanpoil River country, where I was headed. In some of the meadows the huckleberry leaves were turning red. It was the last week of August and summer was beginning to fade in the high country. Eventually the trail began to descend and dropped into a beautiful canyon lined with big cliffs. Here a nice, narrow trail hugged the steep slopes high above the canyon floor before descending to the Thirteenmile Trailhead in Sanpoil Canyon. Three miles/4.8 kilometres on the highway through the canyon followed but little traffic and the splendid scenery, with massive cliffs rising either side, made it one of the pleasanter paved road walks. For a while I watched a bald eagle circling high over the cliffs. I left the highway and the Sanpoil River for the Tenmile Trail, which climbed above the canyon and gave good views back over it before heading away through the forest to link up with some forest roads that took me down to Swan Lake, where I stayed on the Forest Service campground. I'd carried water the last few miles, intending to camp at the first suitable spot. None had appeared and suddenly I'd found the campground in front of me, with water on tap. It cost $8, only the second time I'd paid for a site, the first being at Polebridge,

which now seemed a long, long time ago. Swan Lake was beautiful and serene. Out on the water I heard the wild, thrilling long drawn-out cry of a common loon, or great northern diver, as it's known in Britain, one of my favourite bird calls as it conjures up wild places.

The Kettle Range was behind me now. It had lived up to Ron's description and I'd been very impressed. I was surprised there was no statutory protection for the area, as there wasn't for most of the Selkirk Mountains just to the east, so I was pleased to learn that there is a campaign for the preservation and restoration of the area, run by the organisation Conservation Northwest, which calls the combined Kettle-Selkirk area the Columbia Highlands. Amongst a mass of proposals in the Columbia Highlands Initiative are ones for wilderness areas that would encompass the Kettle Crest Trail, the San Poil – Thirteenmile Trail area and, further back along the PNT, the Abercrombie Mountain area. The Initiative looks well researched and there's an excellent website. A photographic book, *Columbia Highlands: Exploring Washington's Last Frontier* with words by Craig Romano, shows the beauty and majesty of the area well. I hope the campaign is successful as the landscape and its wildlife deserve protecting.

Camp on the slopes of Bald Mountain, Kettle River Range

I was now on the edge of the area known as the Okanogan. This is a dry area of rolling hills and vast meadows where sagebrush and cows are common and water scarce. First I had a somewhat frustrating and tedious day on a selection of roads. It began badly when I couldn't get away from Swan Lake, which was both annoying and ridiculous. On my first attempt I forgot my hat and had to go back for it. A nearby camper asked me where I was going. He'd not hiked any of the PNT but in the past had done some of the Appalachian Trail, including its highest peak, Mount Washington in the White Mountains of New Hampshire, which he said had been very cold in June. I'd climbed it in October and it had been snowing. I could believe it was cold in the summer. The camper told me the forecast was for hotter weather but that the weather had been odd this year with a late spring and two summer rains. Usually the summer was dry throughout, he said, and the rain was not good for the wheat harvest further south. The Okanogan was likely to be the hottest section of the walk anyway. Just not too hot, I hoped.

My second attempt at leaving Swan Lake ended when I couldn't find the route and ended up doing some desperate bushwhacking in dense undergrowth. I was searching for a forest road

Piped spring on the Kettle Crest Trail

on the guidebook route but there was no sign of it. Navigating with the GPS I crossed the line of it twice and couldn't tell there'd ever been a road

The Grand Canyon of the Sanpoil River

there. This was before I even reached the cross-country section described in the guidebook. After too much time thrashing around in the bushes I gave up and returned to the lake, following roads to intersect the PNT some two miles/3.2 kilometres further along, a route that Li had sensibly marked on the map. There followed a day of hot dusty dirt roads in pleasant forest but with only a few views. Happily there were few vehicles. One was a pick-up driven by a rancher who was out checking on his cattle. He stopped to talk, telling me hikers were rare here, which didn't surprise me. It wasn't inspiring country. He had 75 head of cattle in the forest here, which he'd brought up in May and would take down in early October before the snow came. It can get down to -20°F here in winter he told me. I was also passed by a maintenance vehicle with blades like a giant lawnmower that slashed down the young trees and bushes beside the road. It looked quite terrifying, an industrial monster mowing down nature.

I'd finished my paperback books but I did have my smartphone on which I'd downloaded some free novels. In sunlight I couldn't see the screen but in shady areas I walked along reading Robert Louis Stevenson's *Treasure Island*, the classic pirate story that is the template for all the pirate adventures that have followed, in films as well as novels, and which has one of the great villains in literature in the pirate leader, Long John Silver. Reading Stevenson I remembered his words from his book about a long journey, *Travels With A Donkey In The Cevennes*: 'For my part, I travel not to go anywhere, but to go. I travel for travel's sake. The great affair is to move.' I wasn't sure about that, especially not during this dull road walk. I travelled to see and experience. Not to go anywhere but rather to be somewhere. I had music on the phone too, intended for air travel and hotels. I tried listening to this as I walked but it was too distracting. I've met hikers who listen to music regularly on the trail but I just hated being cut off from the sounds of the world around me. I only tried it because I was bored with the roads, heat and lack of views and needed distraction from my hot sore feet.

With no water on the roads I'd decided to camp at the Sweat Creek Campground, where the PNT crossed a highway. However when I got there at dusk a sign said it was now just a picnic spot and closed to camping. The PNT continued beside Sweat Creek on a trail. The creek and its environs had been trampled into filthy mush by cattle – on the map Li had written 'flowing, bovine playground'. Wandering up the trail by headlamp I eventually found a reasonable clean and dry spot amongst big Douglas firs. I had to take water from the creek, filtering it through a bandanna before boiling it.

Swan Lake, Kettle River Range

From Sweat Creek the trail ran over 5400 foot/1646 metre Clackamas Mountain, a big hill with many open meadows giving good views of the rolling Okanogan Highlands. The map showed five springs on the 7.5 mile/12 kilometre crossing of Clackamas, which was promising. However, four of the springs were dry, though two of them had muddy cow-trampled puddles nearby, and I couldn't find the fifth. The water from Sweat Creek would have to do. There were multiple cow paths scouring the slopes of the mountain, which made the actual foot trail difficult to follow in places. I was misled twice. Eventually the trail led off the mountain and down to Cougar Creek, which was flowing vigorously with welcome clear water. I then had a walk on a forest road down the Cougar Creek valley past several areas of dumped cars. This walk was quite shady but it was followed by over 3 miles/5 kilometres uphill on a paved highway straight into the sun with no shade, which was awful. Near the end of this unpleasant road walk I came on a big sign headed 'Bonny Braes', which told how a John Laurie and family had settled here. Laurie had run a sawmill and in 1915 had built a big house here. There was no mention of Scotland on the sign but Laurie is a Scottish name as is 'Bonny Braes' ('brae' being Scots and meaning

a hillside or slope) so I guessed he was a Scottish immigrant. There is nothing left of the house now. Behind the sign there was just a gentle hillside covered in long brown grass waving gently in the breeze. As I looked at the sign two heavily laden cycle tourers pulled up. Sue and Bruce were from Colorado and cycling from Glacier National Park to Seattle and then on down the coast. It had taken them two weeks to reach here. Walking had taken me 36 days.

At the point where the PNT left the highway for a dusty track a pick-up stopped and the driver directed me on the right route, saying he owned all the land hereabouts. More forest roads led through heavily logged country to the hills above Bonaparte Lake. Despite the ragged, damaged forest there were many mule deer, more than I'd seen anywhere else. I found water in a black plastic shaft sunk in the ground, which I guessed was a spring protected from cattle. The water was murky and again I filtered it through a bandanna and boiled it. I camped nearby on the edge of the road, a functional site. Another squirrel chattering loudly just outside the tent woke me at dawn. The temperature was a warm 14°C/57°F. From below I could hear a loon calling on Bonaparte Lake. For breakfast I ate the last of my food – some granola.

All that was left was some dried milk and sugar. I could make sweet milky drinks if necessary.

Half an hour after breaking camp I was down at Bonaparte Lake, and soon afterwards I reached the Bonaparte Lake Resort and a welcome Café sign. The outside of the building was somewhat ramshackle with a curious collection of rural artefacts and a crudely daubed name board. Inside it was warm, homely and welcoming with good music playing – the Grateful Dead and then Bob Marley. It was mainly a fishing store, serving anglers on Bonaparte Lake, and had very limited food supplies, though plenty of fishing lures. I ended up with two cans of baked beans – one for dinner that evening and one for breakfast the next morning – plus candy bars for the day and sachets of hot chocolate for drinks. I hadn't carried cans in decades but nothing but candy for dinner and breakfast didn't appeal. The café offered much more for hikers than the store and I had a good cooked breakfast, relishing eggs again, and plenty of coffee.

From Bonaparte Lake the PNT climbed over big wooded Bonaparte Mountain, an uneventful and pleasant walk apart from one navigational error when I descended the wrong trail for half a mile/1 kilometre and several hundred feet, which

Bonaparte Lake Resort

cost me an hour of time and a fair amount of effort and sweat on what was a hot day. Once over the mountain the route left the woods for Okanogan sagebrush, hay meadows and cattle pastures, and roads, roads, roads, too many roads. Hot, dusty and thirsty I plodded up the Eden Valley looking for a shallow pond where Li had marked a campsite on his map. I never saw the pool but the land next to the road here was posted private and visible from nearby houses so I wandered on wondering where I was going to camp. I checked the map. A side road led through the private land and into the Okanogan National Forest. The road had a private sign but it was after dark so I went anyway, feeling relieved when I passed the forest boundary and then even more relieved when I found a tiny trickle of a creek and some flat ground. I heated the baked beans and ate them straight from the can. They tasted surprisingly good, a nice change from dehydrated meals. I then rinsed the last of the tomato sauce from the can, flattened it and stored it in an old plastic food packet for carrying out.

This was a fairly low level camp at around 3500 feet/1050 metres and quite sheltered so I was surprised to wake feeling a little chilly with the quilt draped loosely over me as usual. I glanced at the thermometer. Just below freezing at -0.6°C/31°F, which made it the coldest night of the walk so far, just twenty-four hours after one of the warmest. Oroville was now just a fairly forgettable 14 mile/22.5 kilometre road walk away. I was there by early afternoon. The weather was thankfully quite cool, chilly enough for me to wear my fleece sweater and long pants for the first few hours. The forecast was for it to remain cool with showers for several days, which should see me through the rest of the Okanogan and back in the mountains.

First though I had two days in Oroville. I'd arrived on a Friday and didn't have enough time to sort everything out and have my mail ready before the Post Office closed until Monday. This wasn't due to bad planning but rather a lack of planning. My itinerary hadn't been detailed enough to give the exact dates at which I expected to reach anywhere. I'd have found that too restrictive. Rather than disappointed at an enforced two day break I was pleased I'd arrived in time to collect my mail, especially my supply box. A few hours later and I'd have had a two day wait and then a third day sorting everything out. I could easily rationalise the need for the time off anyway. I had a 300 mile/483 kilometre section coming up that would take me right through the Cascade Mountains. I expected it to take around 18 days and I wasn't planning on any rest days. I had sent food supplies ahead to the Ross Lake Resort, a remote fishing resort, so I would only need to set off with the first nine days' worth, which was quite enough. On the walk to Oroville I could see the eastern edge of the Cascades rising up above the Okanogan. I was looking forward to reaching them.

Oroville was named in the late nineteenth century after the gold mines in the area – 'oro' being the Spanish for gold. Today agriculture is the main industry, with many orchards in and around the town. From its height of 10,000 during the mining era the population has dwindled to around 1600. Like the other towns along the more remote parts of the PNT to the east of the Cascades Oroville had a slightly decayed air with many closed stores but was also friendly with all the services a hiker could need. I checked into a motel, which was also a bit run-down, especially with regard to the shower which failed to produce more than lukewarm water. Unusually it had wi-fi, though this was intermittent. However the library had computers and I used one to write a report for TGO magazine, send emails and update my blog and Facebook page. Oroville did have good eating places – always a plus point for long distance hikers. I tried several, just to make sure – the Hometown Pizza & Pasta,

Okanogan farmland

Fat Boys Diner and Expressions Espresso all kept me content. There were two supermarkets, so resupplying with more sensible hiking food than baked beans was easy, but no bookshop. However I found a store selling a handful of second books. I prefer to read books about local history or nature during a walk but could find nothing like that so I ended up with the second two volumes in the Lord of the Rings trilogy, favourite books that I knew so well I didn't need the first one. They would keep me entertained during any dull road walks or evenings in the tent in bad weather. Strangely, I couldn't find any postcards, which I'd planned on sending to various friends.

The Post Office produced a mound of mail – my box, a new pack from GoLite (yippee!), a new pair of trail shoes (my second pair), maps from Li and guidebook pages from Kris. The pack was a different model, weighing slightly more but designed for heavier loads. I'd send the old one back to GoLite when the Post Office opened so they could have a look and see what was wrong. (In fact, although I did this the pack never arrived so I never did discover the cause of the problems). Late on the first evening in Oroville a flurry of emails suddenly arrived on my phone from my partner Denise. I felt relieved. It was wonderful to hear from her. Although I had sent her quite a few emails I'd not had much in the way of replies. She'd been sending them though, but to the wrong address. I'd acquired a new one for travelling and this had caused some confusion, which was my fault for not making things clear. I was glad to hear that Denise was fine and enjoying the Edinburgh Festival, which we'd visited together the previous three years.

Dry sagebrush country in the Okanagan

CHAPTER 5

STORMS IN THE CASCADES

OROVILLE TO SEDRO WOOLLEY

August 30 – September 16

300 miles/483 km

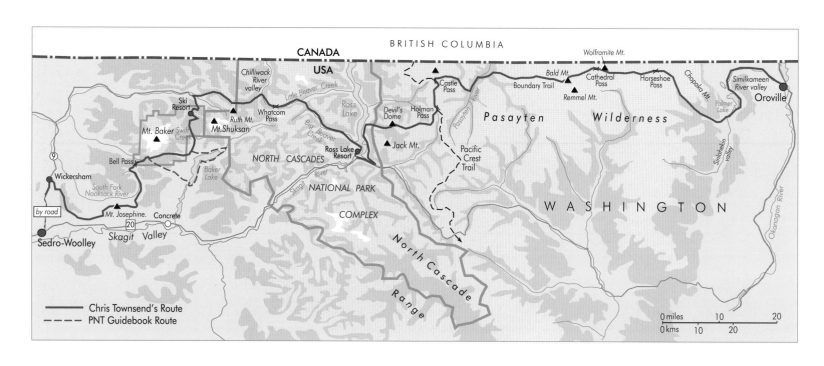

Chris Townsend's Route
PNT Guidebook Route

After two days of shopping, eating, sorting, eating, writing, eating and resting I was ready to return to the trail. I was also excited. I had been anticipating this section of the trail since I set off. As well as being the longest section between towns it was also the longest in protected wild areas without logging or roads and it went through the magnificent Cascades, one of the most rugged mountain ranges in the USA. First though, I had to finish crossing the Okanogan and climb back up to the high country, which would take me two days.

The first day was a footsore road walk with a heavy pack. As well as 9 days food I had 2 litres of alcohol stove fuel as there would be nowhere to resupply until the end of this section and I didn't want to rely on wood as wet weather was likely in the Cascades. The new pack was comfortable though and I was relieved to have it. The PNT left Oroville along the Similkameen River valley. There is an old railway line along this valley and the plan is that the PNT will run along this rather than the paved highway. However, at the time of my hike, agreements hadn't been made with private landowners whose land had to be crossed to reach the old railway, which is a legal right of way. Whilst a short bit of trespassing has never bothered me (or even a long bit on some occasions in the past)

doing so here could make efforts to secure access rights harder so I reluctantly stuck to the road. To emphasise the point a large sign on a wire fence put up by Okanogan County showed where the trail will hopefully go and firmly commanded 'Do Not Proceed Beyond This Point'.

The road soon left farmland for sagebrush

and creosote bush dotted bluffs alongside the winding river, an unusual landscape for the PNT. A sign headed 'Shankars Bend/Rich Bar' said that the first gold in the area was discovered here in 1859. The map showed old mines on the hills above the river – King Solomon, Alice, Kabba Texas, Four Metals, Wyandote and more. This must have

Pasayten Wilderness sign, Cascade Mountains

Upper Cathedral Peak, Pasayten Wilderness, Cascade Mountains

been a busy industrial area at one time. Now it's just sagebrush and dust. Ahead the great walls of Chopaka and Grandview Mountains rose out of the brown hills. As road walks went this one wasn't too bad. The landscape was interesting, there was little traffic and, surprisingly, the weather was quite cool. Several times I watched mule deer bouncing away through the sagebrush. There was no other wildlife.

Suddenly, as I was walking along the road paying little attention to the occasional vehicle, a large SUV pulled up across my path. 'Border Patrol' it said on the side. A uniformed officer got out. His companion was on the radio. Shortly afterwards two more SUVs pulled up. I was surrounded by four armed border patrol officers. Who are you, where are you going, where have you come from, why are you here? They were polite but firm. I explained and produced my passport. The officers relaxed, accepting that I wasn't a terrorist or drug smuggler who had slipped across the Canadian border. Soon we were having a friendly chat and they were showing interest in my walk. I ended up posing for photos with them (a good way to get a photo of me of course, not that I objected). The whole episode was quite surreal and did add some interest to what despite the scenery was not the most stimulating day.

As the border patrol climbed back into their vehicles the skies darkened and rain began to fall. Soon after they'd departed in search of other suspicious characters the rain became a cloudburst. In just sandals, shorts and shirt I was quickly soaked to the skin, except for my head, protected by my faithful Tilley Hat. I wasn't cold though and so plodded on soggily to Palmer Lake. Here I stopped at a free well-used campground run by the Washington State Department of Natural Resources on a narrow strip of land between the road and the lake. Most of the sites were taken but I found a space just big enough for my tent

Storm during the climb out of the Okanagon to the eastern Cascades

under a big ponderosa pine. Bits of fish lay round about; skin, bones and flesh. I guessed bears were unlikely to be a problem. There were outhouses but no taps so I boiled water from the lake, suspecting it might not be too clean as there were houses and businesses along the banks.

'A Scottish day', I wrote in my journal the next morning. The harsh calls of jays and gulls had woken me at dawn; scavengers looking for scraps of campers' food. The sky was overcast and there was a gusty south wind with hints of rain in it. Waves on the lake lapping on the pebble shore sounded like the sea. For the first time on the walk I adopted a bad weather stratagem from home –

linger in the tent over a hot drink and hope for an improvement. No-one else in the campground was moving either. As so often with this ploy it failed and the weather stayed dismal. Eventually I stirred myself and set off, feeling uninspired. The weather remained overcast and cool all day with the clouds hiding the summits. There was on and off drizzle and a few light showers but never enough that I needed waterproofs. Long pants and my windproof jacket were essential though. This was not what I expected from the Okanogan

Walking beside Palmer Lake I watched an osprey flying over the water and a loon floating on it, nice distractions from the road. Then it was across the fields of the wide Sinlahekin Valley to warm up on the long climb up the steep Chopaka Grade Road, a gravel track that gave good views back along the valley to Palmer Lake. The scenery was pleasant, probably excellent if the high peaks had been visible, but the road walking was tedious again and I was on dirt roads all day. The Chopaka Grade led up into the forest, here state owned with much of it logged and cow trodden. As I climbed higher I noticed the remnants of a recent snowfall amongst the trees. A jeep passed me as I approached Cold Spring Campground at the end of the road. Two big recreational vehicles were parked in the

The old Tungsten Mine on Wolframite Mountain

campground with a large campfire between them. The jeep pulled up and the two occupants waved me over to the fire. They were up here for several days grouse shooting. This was the fifteenth visit at this time of year for one of them and he said he'd never known it to rain before, let alone snow. Drizzle fell all evening but I kept warm by the fire, drinking beer with the grouse hunters and talking about many subjects including falconry, on which one of them was an expert. They had a pointer dog that took a great liking to me, as dogs often do.

The road end just beyond the campground was the gateway to the Pasayten Wilderness, a vast area covering 530,000 acres of the eastern North Cascades that was designated an official wilderness area in 1968. This is a high mountain wilderness with peaks rising to over 9,000 feet/2740 metres and an average height of 5,500 feet/1675 metres. I'd traversed the western side of the Pasayten on the Pacific Crest Trail 28 years earlier, mostly in wet and stormy weather and I was looking forward to seeing it again, hopefully in clearer, drier conditions. The Pasayten is rich in wildlife, with even a few wolves and grizzly bears, plus old growth forest with magnificent giant trees. Like the rest of the Cascades the geology of the Pasayten is complex, with volcanic, metamorphic and sedimentary rocks

all present. The Cascades are young mountains, the result of the clash of tectonic plates in the Pacific Ocean with the American plate, which some eight million years ago started to push the mountains upwards. The ice ages then sculpted the Cascades as we see them today; with continuing weathering and volcanic eruptions still changing the mountains, sometimes violently in the case of the latter.

Initially I was still in country with signs of much logging and cattle grazing. The Chopaka Mountain Trail led through the woods from the campground to Swamp Creek and some nasty clear-cuts. This area is protected now but it will take many decades for the scars to heal and even longer for the ecosystem to be restored. There is road access up the Swamp Creek valley and I met some day walkers here – hiking without even day packs – heading for Snowshoe Cabin, a dilapidated tin-roofed hut. Continuing across the big meadows of Goodenough Park, mostly on cow paths, I had good views of Horseshoe Mountain up ahead. The day was clear but cold with a north-west wind and again I was hiking in long pants and windproof jacket. Then, just before the summit of Goodenough Peak, I reached the wilderness boundary, marked by a sign and a barbed wire fence crossed by a stile.

Upper Cathedral Lake, Pasayten Wilderness, Cascade Mountains

No more cows! No more logging! I felt a surge of excitement and enthusiasm. It had been a long ten days since I'd come down from the Kettle River

Range. Finally I was back in the mountains again, and this time I would stay in them and in the wilderness for many days to come.

Passing below rugged Arnold Peak I crossed Horseshoe Basin to broad 7006 foot/2135 metre Horseshoe Pass where there were many campsites. The country here was mostly open meadows with scattered groves of trees and splendid views of big mountains rising high above timberline. A solo backpacker with a big pack stopped to chat. Jan had planned to be out for nine days but was cutting it to six due to the stormy weather of the last two days. She said on the first of these there had been several inches of snow that made the trail finding difficult and this was followed by a day of constant rain.

From the pass the Boundary Trail wound across the slopes high above the Horseshoe Creek valley. To the west I could see jagged peaks. I camped on a col not far from a curving wall of rock called Teapot Dome. The peaks of the Eastern Pasayten are built of granite and other igneous rocks and Teapot and similar glacier-sliced and smoothed domes are reminiscent of the granite domes of Yosemite far to the south in California.

My camp was at 6880 feet/2097 metres amongst lodgepole pines and subalpine firs and the night was cold and clear so it wasn't a surprise when I woke to a temperature of -1.1°C/30°F. The tent, which had still been wet from the rain at Cold Spring Campground when I pitched it, was frozen stiff and coated white with frost and for the first time on the walk there was ice in my water bottles. I sipped a warming mix of coffee and hot chocolate as I watched the sun creeping down the slopes to the west and then touching distant tree tops. In my shadowed camp it was cold but I knew that soon the sun would reach me and the temperature would rise rapidly. My breakfast was honey and almond granola from a supermarket in Oroville. At least that's what it claimed to be. I couldn't taste honey or almonds or much of anything. I added raisins and sugar and it was still boring. Dull food couldn't detract from the glorious situation though. Still huddled under the quilt I made another hot drink. The sun reached the top of the subalpine fir directly in front of the tent. Then, an hour and a half after I'd wakened, the sun touched the tent and the frozen moisture began to thaw and run and drip. It was time to get up. I hung the tent on a tree to dry and spread out other items to air while I watched the mountains and the sky, revelling at being back in the wilds. The day ahead looked so wonderful I was reluctant to start for fear it couldn't live up to my expectations.

I needn't have been concerned. The day was indeed marvellous, with one section being the best three miles/5 kilometres of the walk so far. From my camp the trail wound round the slopes of Bauerman Ridge high above forested valleys that stretched out to the south. Up here the forest was open and scattered with many small meadows so the vistas were extensive and continuous. As Ron wrote in the guidebook 'the views keep coming'. Dropping into slightly denser forest below Wolframite Mountain I reached the remains of the Tungsten Mine, which was worked from the 1900s to the 1940s. The mineral wolframite is the main source of tungsten, hence the names of both mountain and mine. I looked round the mine cabins. Although somewhat rickety they were in reasonable condition and could be used for accommodation in stormy weather. Below them the old mine workings and accompanying detritus littered the mountainside making a real, though I guess historic, mess.

Across Tungsten Creek I could see the big rocky east face of Apex Mountain. The trail led round the head of the creek to Apex Pass at 7280 feet/2219 metre. From the pass I looked out on a magnificent mountain landscape with the huge

Remmel Mountain, Pasayten Wilderness, Cascade Mountains

curving rock walls of Amphitheatre Mountain sweeping round to the great ragged fang of Cathedral Peak. From the pass the trail swung round the head of Cathedral Creek and then passed right under the huge walls of Cathedral Peak to Cathedral Pass at 7580 feet/2310 metres, which made it the high point of the walk so far. This walk between the two passes was *the* superlative three miles, a perfect mountain hike.

The approach to Cathedral Pass was over rocky slopes above a steep, rugged bowl; a harsh, austere landscape. The pass was no narrow notch in a mountain wall however but a stony saddle sloping away gently westwards to broad meadows dotted with tree groves and pools; a much softer scene. On the edge of the meadows I could see Upper Cathedral Lake nestling under the screes and rock walls of the western spur of Amphitheatre Mountain while beyond the meadows green forest stretched out to distant peaks, some of them white with snow and ice. Here on the eastern edge of the Cascades the mountains are spread out and there is a sense of vastness and space. Further west I knew the peaks were tangled together and the sense was of depth and height rather than distance. I sat and studied the landscape, my back against a rough boulder. Soon though mosquitoes, the most voracious for many days, persuaded me I should move on.

Camp on Bald Mountain, Pasayten Wilderness, Cascade Mountains

The trail wound across to Upper Cathedral Lake and a dramatic view across the water to snow-spattered, shattered cliffs. There were camp sites here and it was a lovely spot but it was too early to stop and I was enjoying the walking too much. The weather and landscape were both perfect. I didn't want the day to end. Beyond the lake a big boulder field gave the roughest walking since the Selkirk Crest many weeks earlier, a nice contrast to the meadow trails. Still on the Boundary Trail that I had joined on Horseshoe Pass I wandered across another plateau of meadows, pools and groves.

Across the meadows the triangular rock peak of Remmel Mountain rose into a sky now streaked attractively with fine, wispy clouds. Beautiful though the scene was I knew those clouds could well be the leading edge of a storm system.

At a creek I filled my water containers, loading my pack down with an extra 3 litres as the guidebook suggested there might be no water for a while and I wanted to camp high up, before the next descent. I then passed seven water sources in the next few miles! So much must depend on what the weather has been like and the time of year. With unseasonal rain and snow just a few days before it perhaps wasn't surprising that there was water in places that were usually dry in the summer.

The trail now traversed the northern slopes of long Bald Mountain before climbing onto the north-west shoulder, where a big meadow stretched out to the distant summit. Here I camped, out in the open, high on the mountain at 7,000 feet/2134 metres. A gusty wind swept over the grasses. For once the tent would have to show its wind resistance, but a camp here, high in the heart of the wilderness with the vastness of the natural world spread out all around me, was not to be missed. It was a grand camp to end a grand day.

View across the Pasayten River valley to the central Cascades, Pasayten Wilderness

The wind woke me twice during the night. Holding my anemometer out of the tent I recorded a gust of 18.5mph/30kph, which wasn't that strong. At home I often camped in windier weather, but I had become used to quiet camps in the woods with no wind to rustle the tent. Now even a wind like this could disturb me. Before dawn the sky was overcast but the clouds were dissipating as the first light coloured the sky. Five mule deer were grazing quietly not far away. I sat outside the tent over breakfast, looking back at Cathedral Peak and Amphitheatre Mountain, which would remain long in my mind.

Since I'd climbed back up into the mountains

three days before the trail had stayed high with little in the way of ascent or descent, making the walking easy and effortless. This changed beyond Bald Mountain with a 2000 foot/610 metre descent down steep switchbacks to the Ashnola River followed by an equally long and steep climb back up to the southern slopes of Sheep Mountain. Ashnola River was spanned by a single log bridge with a wire hand rail. My feet were hot so I ignored it and paddled across barefoot; the cold water making my feet feel wonderfully refreshed. There were many dusty well-used campsites by the crossing along with a lean-to wooden shelter. This would be a good place for a camp in stormy weather I thought but the heights were far better when it was fine.

Once I'd reached Sheep Mountain the day became another splendid one of spacious vistas from a succession of fine subalpine meadows as I crossed Peeves Pass, skirted Sand Ridge, traversed the slopes of Quartz Mountain and climbed Bunker Hill. There were still some flowers – lupin, paintbrush – in the meadows but also red autumn tints on some leaves. To the west the long ragged line of alpine mountains along the Cascade Crest held my eye. The view was especially good from 7239 foot/2206 metre Bunker Hill, my first summit in the Pasayten Wilderness. Not far beyond this

mountain the Boundary Trail, which I was still following, began a long descent to the Pasayten River. Wanting another high camp I dropped a little way into a bowl on the side of Bunker Hill and pitched the tent on the edge of a little meadow at the headwaters of Bunker Hill Creek. The guidebook described this as an 'excellent, grassy campsite'

and others had obviously thought so as it was marred just a little by the presence of fire rings and blackened rocks. I sat outside cooking over wood under a magnificent starry sky. It had been another magical wilderness day.

The early morning was chilly and I sat wrapped in my quilt over breakfast. Then I plunged

Attempting to dry footwear and socks at the Canyon Creek camp, Pasayten Wilderness

Burnt forest and fireweed in the Pasayten River valley

into the dense forest for the long descent to the Pasayten River. The trees soon opened out though, as a huge fire had burned most of them and there were views through the blackened remnants across fireweed covered ground. Down in the valley I found the Pasayten River Trail blocked off and with no sign it had been maintained recently. I followed the trail anyway – there wasn't any choice – and forded the East Fork and the main river in sandals. Both were shallow. The forest was still burned along the river. In total I was in the dead forest for five hours. Despite the colourful ground cover provided by the masses of tall pink-purple fireweed, which, as the name suggests, colonises burned areas, it was a little eerie and I felt relieved to reach Soda Creek and live green trees. Li had obviously felt something similar as he'd written on the map 'blissfully unburned'.

At Soda Creek I left the river to pass through a flat area packed with small lodgepole pines that had once been a backcountry airstrip and then begin the long climb back to the high country. West of the Pasayten River the terrain changed. I'd left the big flat high level meadows and widely spaced peaks behind. Now the more heavily glaciated peaks were on long narrow ridges rising above deep, steep-sided valleys.

As I climbed beside Soda and then Frosty Creek the day became cooler and windier with clouds sweeping across the once blue sky. Because of the weather I stopped at Frosty Lake, where there was a big well-used campsite, so I could camp in the shelter of the trees. The guidebook described it as an 'unattractive horse camp'. There was a big fire ring and some cut wood but no litter. I'd camped in less attractive places.

Despite the sheltered site I had a disturbed night for two very different reasons. The first was rain, which began about half past midnight, with the noise on the tent and the drops blowing onto me through the open door. The rain was thin and

Pacific Crest Trail sign, Pasayten Wilderness

Western Red Cedar along the Big Beaver Trail, North Cascades National Park

light, the drops small and cold. When I woke again at 2.30am it had stopped. This time it was hard ground under me that was the cause. My airbed was flat. I blew it up and sank back to sleep. An hour later it was flat again, which meant a puncture. I blew it up again and managed to sleep three hours before the lack of cushioning woke me again. At least the ground wasn't cold, though looking out I could see frost in the nearby meadow.

Needing to find the leak I took the mat down to the lake and discovered it was almost impossible to wrestle an inflated airbed into water, which I needed to do so I could look for tell-tale bubbles from the leak. Drizzle fell and I could see fresh snow dusting the mountains above. My arms, submerged in the cold water, were going numb. Unable to sink the whole mat I ended up holding sections of it down in the water and then squeezing them so they were under enough pressure to force any air out. As the lake was too shallow at the edge I did this balancing on a log out in deeper water. Finally after half an hour or more as I squeezed one end of the mat I heard a hiss and spotted the bubbles. I could now end this ridiculous performance. Relieved I turned to return to the shore and promptly slipped, getting both feet wet and sinking into foul-smelling mud to my knees.

Now I would have wet shoes for a high level walk that might be in snow. I was not in a good mood. A duck with a duckling watched me from out on the lake, as did a dipper from a rock. Why my thrashing about in the water hadn't scared them away I had no idea. Maybe my bizarre behaviour was providing entertainment. Back at the tent I slid back under the quilt to warm my feet and drank some hot coffee while I patched the mat. Would it hold? I would find out the next night.

The day to come was one I had been looking forward to since I planned the walk as I would climb up to the Pacific Crest Trail and follow the section of this on the Cascade Crest where I had seen nothing due to bad weather when I hiked that trail so long ago. I set off hoping for sunshine and not too much rain, snow or mist. It was not to be. That evening I wrote in my journal 'a short, strange, cathartic and, I think, important day'.

It began with a climb in light drizzle up avalanche slopes to a big bowl below Winthrop Mountain. At one point I stopped to check the map. Not much further along I saw something moving high in the bowl. Through binoculars I could see three bears amongst clumps of huckleberries. A mother with two large cubs, I guessed. I watched them closely. They had clear shoulder humps.

Grizzlies! These were very rare in this area but I was pretty certain I was right. These were not black bears. This was exciting and my mood improved. Then I discovered I had lost a lens from my reading glasses. I'd used them when I looked at the map. I retraced my steps but couldn't find it. I cursed my carelessness and mentally thanked Kris who had suggested I should carry some cheap reading glasses as spares. As I stared helplessly about, hoping to spot the lens, an excited hiker came down the trail. He'd seen the bears and been delighted.

I climbed onto Frosty Pass, where it began to hail, and then descended steep switchbacks to Castle Pass where the hail turned back to drizzle. Here I joined the Pacific Crest Trail, soon spotting a familiar metal marker on a tree. I'd linked my two longest walks, the PCT and the Continental Divide Trail, which gave me a brief feeling of pleasure. Ahead was potentially one of the most spectacular sections of the whole walk. What I had though were dripping trees, wet brush soaking my legs and mountains hidden in cloud. I felt inordinately disappointed. I really wanted to see this landscape. Plodding along the trail with cold, wet feet I felt disillusioned for the first time on the walk. Even on the hot road walks in ruined forest I hadn't felt like this. A mass of worries surfaced. Concerns from

Big Beaver Creek, North Cascades National Park

home, concerns about the walk, concerns about my eyes now I'd lost that lens. The negative feelings spiralled and expanded, feeding on each other. Suddenly the whole walk seemed pointless. Why was I doing it? There had been too much effort for too few rewards and I felt pressurised to keep moving. Where was the enjoyment? My misery grew. I shook myself. Literally. I had to get out of this mood. What should I do? Was I really under so much pressure? I knew the answer; of course not. Why was I feeling like this? I listed the reasons in my mind: a broken night's sleep, the punctured mat, losing the glasses lens and, by far the most important, the disappointment of the weather. Thinking it through a solution came to me and that was to stop and camp. I did have time for a short day. I didn't have a tight schedule. The pressure to keep moving was all in my head. Rest, warmth and hot food and drink were the restoratives I needed.

The decision made I strode on towards the next pass, knowing I could drop down to camp in sheltered forest from there. Two hikers came towards me, looking happy and triumphant. 'Not far to the border', they said. No, I thought, just a few hours away. I assumed they were Pacific Crest Trail hikers finishing their walk from Mexico. I remembered how ecstatic I had felt standing at the

finish in the rain all those years ago. How would I feel at the end of this trail? I wondered.

At Hopkins Pass I dropped down to a partly sheltered campsite amongst the trees. It was only half past one and I'd walked less than six miles/10 kilometres. Soon I was in the tent, warming up my feet in dry socks under the quilt and eating leek soup for lunch. Drizzle continued to drift down. Later in the afternoon I was glad I'd stopped early as there was a violent hailstorm. The noise on the tent was tremendous and the ground turned white. There followed rapidly changing weather with showers, some heavy, of rain, more hail and snow with very short bursts of blue sky and sunshine between them. I checked the maps. It was around 45 miles/72 kilometres to the Ross Lake Resort where my supply box should be waiting. I should be there in three days and I had ample food left. Lying in the tent I brought my journal up to date, including my moans of earlier in the day, read some Tolkien and then, fed up of listening to the rain drumming on the tent, I put on some music. The gravelly voices of Tom Waits and Howlin' Wolf seemed to fit the situation. 'The weather vane will say/It smells like rain today' sang Waits in his laid back song *Green Grass*. The Wolf, meanwhile, was having an exciting *All Night Boogie,* backed by

Willie Johnson's wonderful, exuberant, wild guitar.

I was asleep early and I slept long – ten hours, broken only briefly when heavy rain woke me sometime in the night. Maybe tiredness had been the main cause of the previous day's negativity. I hoped it wasn't the weather as the sky was still overcast. A breeze rippled round the dark and sombre Engelmann's spruce trees that I was camped amongst. The mat had stayed inflated so my repair had been effective.

Climbing back up to Hopkins Pass I entered the cloud and I stayed in it most of the rest of the day as I headed south along the Pacific Crest Trail. Rain fell on and off all day, turning to snow on the higher sections. This stuck to the trees giving them a wintry look. The landscape was mysterious and ethereal, hazy views of deep valleys, big cliffs, dark lakes and pale snowfields fading in and out of the swirling cloud. The air was cold as well as wet. For the first time on the walk I wore my waterproof jacket and waterproof trousers all day. As I followed the narrow but clear winding trail I pondered my mood of the previous day. I wasn't used to feeling like that. Only two days earlier I had felt elated at the wilderness and the wonderful walking. I had, I realised, forgotten one lesson that I had learnt long ago and should have remembered. This was

Cable car, Chilliwack River, North Cascades National Park

that nature has to be taken on its own terms and when you venture into the wilds you have to accept what it gives you, which might well mean storms as well as sunshine. A major part of wilderness is that it's uncontrolled and uncontrollable. What you find there is what it is at that time. Here on the Cascade Crest the mist and snow and rain were part of the landscape, part of the wilderness, part of the experience. Walking in wild places shows us how small our place is in nature and how we have to adapt to its moods. I should not have forgotten this.

After the walk several people did say that perhaps I should have noted the name 'Cascades' and expected wet weather. Now, whilst the Cascades are certainly wetter than mountain ranges further east, especially on the western side, they aren't named for the rain that falls. In fact the name comes from the Cascade Rapids (now submerged in a reservoir) on the Columbia River, which cuts through the range along what is now the border between the states of Oregon and Washington and which was a barrier to early explorers. The mountains either side of the river were called 'the mountains by the Cascades' which soon became just 'the Cascades'.

With easy road access from Harts Pass just to the south of the wilderness area and a well-maintained trail this is a popular area. I met seventeen other hikers during the day, some doing the whole PCT in Washington State and some just out for a few days and hiking the trail to the Canadian border and back again. Two asked me if I'd seen their companions as they'd become separated on the trail. In one case the description was clear enough that I could say I had and they weren't far up ahead. At Holman Pass where the PNT leaves the PCT and turns westwards two bedraggled hikers were sheltering under a tree where one was trying to roll a cigarette. They only had short rain jackets and no waterproof trousers and looked at mine with envy. They'd got lost the day before, taking

Hannegan Trailhead, North Cascades

a wrong turn and climbing towards the Cascade Crest rather than descending into the valley. They knew where they were now and had decided to head out via Harts Pass.

Leaving the PCT I hiked down the Devil's Ridge Trail to Canyon Creek where there were some sheltered campsites in a pleasant spot under big subalpine firs and close to the trickling creek. This would do for the day I decided, although it was early and I'd only walked 11 miles/18 kilometres. In this weather I didn't feel like pushing on. The two hikers I'd met at Holman Pass had camped here the previous night and had told me they'd constructed a drying rack over a campfire to try and dry some of their wet clothing. Their crude but effective contraption of bent branches was still there and as the rain had stopped I lit a small fire under it and smoked my socks and shoes, which had now been sodden for two days. Heavy rain soon returned however so the fire didn't last long and my footwear stayed wet. I was lying in the tent staring out at the rain and drinking hot chocolate just as the light was fading when two hikers came past. They stopped briefly to say hello and told me they were hiking the Pacific Northwest Trail, the first PNT hikers I'd met, and as it would turn out the only ones I would meet. They had the trail names

'Pepper' and 'Nacho', which I presume were given them on the Appalachian Trail which seems to be the source of such names – and part of the reason I've never had a trail name, which are always given by other hikers, as I've never hiked it. Pepper and Nacho had come all the way from the Pasayten River that day and were going on another 3 miles/5 kilometres before camping for a total of about 29 miles/47 kilometres. I wouldn't see them again. They said the forecast had been for the weather to clear today and that it was meant to be fine in two days' time. Whilst I wasn't planning such long days as Pepper and Nacho I did want to reach the Ross Lake Resort and collect my supplies in two days' time so I needed to speed up. Most of the way there was along the lakeshore however so I expected the walking to be quite easy.

First I had a final Pasayten Wilderness mountain ridge to traverse. In the guidebook Ron described it as 'splendid, stop-and-stare scenery'. From the brief glimpses I had through the clouds I suspected he was right. Mostly, though, I was hiking in cloud and heavy rain. Indeed, this was the wettest day yet. Over breakfast I had seen some patches of blue sky high above and whiter, brighter clouds. 'Do not be too hopeful!' I ordered myself in my journal. It was a wise command. Mist was drifting through the

forest as I set off along this spur of the main Cascade Crest. Every so often there would be tantalising hints of a clearance with a slight brightening of the gloom, faint shadows and the pale outline of the sun behind thinning clouds. Across the valley to the south rose the highest mountain in the Pasayten, 9066 foot/2763 metre Jack Mountain. I never saw the summit but occasionally I was granted glimpses of the massive Nohokomeen Glacier on its north-west flanks. The trail ran through open meadows where I saw marmots, the first of the walk, and mule deer, and over 6982 foot/2128 metre Devil's Dome, my second and last Pasayten summit. Then it was down the steep Devil's Dome Trail a full 5100 feet/1555 metres of descent. The top of the trail was very overgrown with head-high shrubs in places. It was a relief to reach bigger trees and a less restricted trail.

The trail led to the East Bank Trail above Ross Lake, which is a huge reservoir. I headed along this wide trail to the Rainbow Point Campground. Now I was in the Ross Lake National Recreation Area I needed a permit to camp and could only do so at designated sites, as would be the case in the North Cascades National Park, which I would enter soon. Both are managed by the National Park Service as the North Cascades National Park Complex.

I did have a permit, or at least a permit number, obtained over the phone from Oroville, but I was now one day behind the dates I'd given the ranger. I had explained I couldn't guarantee any dates and she'd said that would be okay. I hoped any rangers I met would agree.

Down by the lake the trees were impressive, big western red cedars and Douglas firs with delicate birches and maples to break the solidity and massiveness of the conifers, and I enjoyed my walk to the campground. The understory was thick and rich here and with moisture dripping from every leaf it definitely had the feel of a rain forest. The campground had picnic tables and bear proof containers for food. Not that I now had much of the latter left. Once I'd eaten dinner there were just two Clif bars and some coffee and hot chocolate powder remaining. I'd walked 20 miles/32 kilometres. Ross Lake Resort and my food supplies were 15 miles/24 kilometres away.

The morning was overcast but dry. The only sound was the lapping of waves on the lakeshore. A mule deer wandered through the campground as I optimistically spread out some damp gear so it could at least air. While nothing had become really wet after three rainy, humid days much of my gear felt a little clammy. The day's walk began with an

uneventful though pleasant forest walk along the East Bank Trail, at first not far above Lake Ross then veering away from the water to climb to Hidden Hand Pass, which lay between two knolls above a long arm of the reservoir stretching up Ruby Creek. Just as I approached the pass a large, dark black bear appeared on the trail coming towards me. Briefly we stared at each other, then it raced off uphill, its clumsy looking gait belied by the speed with which it crashed through the undergrowth and over logs. Watching the bear I was even more certain I had seen grizzlies on the slopes of Winthrop Mountain. This bear was a very different shape. I hadn't thought about those grizzlies since seeing them, the sighting overwhelmed by the other events and feelings of that day. Thinking about them now I realised that watching bears feeding in a meadow, rather than running away as the other bears I'd seen had done, was a privilege whether they were grizzly or black bears. I'd appreciated that at the time then forgotten it. I was glad this bear had reminded me. Those bears were the key event of that otherwise dismal day, not the weather or my minor equipment failures or how I felt.

From the pass the trail descended to a bridge over Ruby Creek, leaving the Pasayten Wilderness after eight days, and then climbed up to a car park

by Highway 20, the first paved road I'd seen since leaving Oroville ten days before. Thankfully the trail didn't follow the road but I did utilise the outhouse and the rubbish bins in the car park before setting off along the Happy Panther Trail, which ran through the narrow strip of woods between the road and the Ruby Creek arm of Ross Lake to the Ross Dam across the Skagit River. This 150 mile/240 kilometre river was the first major river since I'd crossed the Continental Divide in Glacier National Park that wasn't a tributary of the Columbia River. In crossing the Cascade Crest I had finally left the huge Columbia River basin behind. Running north-west of the Columbia the Skagit cuts through the North Cascades to reach salt water at Skagit Bay on Puget Sound. The Skagit would now parallel the PNT for many miles and I would be close to it again.

I couldn't help but admire the curving concrete wall of the dam, which was graceful in its own way. 540-foot/160 metres high and 1,300-foot/400 metres long it's an impressive structure. The reservoir behind the dam stretches 23 miles/37 kilometres across the border into Canada. The dam was built between 1937 and 1949 to provide hydro-electric power for the city of Seattle. There were plans to build the dam even higher, which would have extended the reservoir further into Canada,

Mount Shuksan, North Cascades

but this was defeated by environmentalists in the 1970s. My route led across the dam, from which I could peer down to the remnant river far below. Two seasoned-looking hikers were crossing in the other direction, carrying old faded external frame packs and using long wooden-shafted ice axes as walking sticks. One indicated the camera bag at his waist – 'I see you do the same as us – take pictures of everything.' I concurred. My camera bag was slung across my body as usual.

From the far side of the dam a rough trail led to the fascinating collection of floating cabins and buildings that make up the Ross Lake Resort, to which the only access is by water or trail. A member of the staff told me it had been originally built for loggers when the dam was being constructed and had been a resort since the 1950s. My supply box was there along with two others waiting for collection. I was relieved, particularly as the only supplies the resort had were candy bars, soft drinks and beer, though the friendly staff did give me a tomato and an apple – the first fresh fruit since Oroville. I ate the tomato that evening, the apple the next morning. They both tasted delicious.

I sat outside at a picnic table protected from the rain that had begun to fall by a large umbrella to sort out my box. I was puzzled by some of the contents. Thirteen evening meals seemed a little excessive, especially as the rest of the food was only enough for eight days, which was how long I had thought it would take me to reach the next town. There was a single packet of oatcakes too, but no cheese or spreads to go with them. I'd probably chucked it in at the last minute. I also had all the remaining guidebook pages and maps of the Olympic National Park, which was still a long way ahead. I couldn't send any stuff on from here though so it would all have to be carried. One of the resort guests came over to ask what I was doing. He'd been visiting here every year for 15 years because he liked the peace and quiet and told me it was wet 70% of the time and only sunny for 10%. The forecast said 30% chance of rain the next two days. The resort is mainly for anglers and some came in with a catch while I was there. The guest I spoke to said he just liked going for day hikes and pottering about in a boat.

As the rain was hammering down I enquired about accommodation at the resort but, as I expected, all the cabins were booked so I walked on for half an hour to the first campground on the West Bank Trail, situated on a little headland protruding out into the lake. A large party of young men were already there and had spread themselves over several sites. In the trees above the main part of the site I found a small pitch for my little tent. The group was from the National Outdoor Leadership School (NOLS) and were on an eighty day course, which was longer than my walk. They'd canoed down Ross Lake to here after backpacking in the Pasayten. To come were an ascent of Mount Baker, some rock climbing and finally a sail along the coast near Vancouver Island. One of the youngsters told me how they'd hiked through a blizzard in the Pasayten and then had a 3200 foot/975 metre bushwhacking descent with many blow-downs to cross. It was clear he'd enjoyed both experiences. Later in the evening another large organised party of youngsters, this time female, hiked in. The NOLS group had to reorganise themselves and give up some of their sites. I was acutely aware that I didn't have a permit and shouldn't really be here. My little site wasn't big enough for any of the big 3-4 person tents of the groups though – even my solo one overhung the tent pad – and eventually everyone had enough room.

I lit a fire in the pit provided and looked through my food to decide what to eat. I now had specialist backpacking food and wholefoods bought from the stores in Issaquah before the walk began. I hadn't had stuff like this since the

Log crossing, Rainbow Creek, North Cascades

first week of the walk. I chose a Mountain House Pasta Primavera. It tasted wonderful. My only disappointment was that the only drink in my supply box had been coffee – no hot chocolate, no spiced apple cider – but it did taste far better than the supermarket stuff I'd been drinking. I'd just finished the meal when the rain began again so I retreated to the tent for the night.

Heavy rain battering the tent woke me early. Soon afterwards the NOLS boys started some communal singing. Then the first motor boats from the resort roared down the lake. Breakfast could wait until I was somewhere more peaceful, so I quickly packed and headed off along the trail to Big Beaver Creek, which would take me from Ross Lake into the North Cascades National Park, munching the apple from the resort. This national park is a rugged area with steep alpine mountains and more glaciers – over 300 – than anywhere else in the USA outside Alaska. Most of the park is also designated a wilderness area – the Stephen Mather Wilderness – which gives it extra protection.

My entry into the park along the Big Beaver Creek Trail went through increasingly magnificent forest with the biggest trees I'd seen yet – giant Douglas fir, western red cedar and western hemlock. A fine, fine forest hung with moss and lichen and with dense undergrowth below the trees. It felt ancient and eternal. I felt privileged to be here. With such a forest to walk through I didn't mind if I couldn't see the mountains. Soon the sounds of Ross Lake vanished and I was alone in a silent, primeval world. Just once I heard a faint splash and saw a canoe moving slowly up the creek with a man in the rear quietly paddling and a man in the front with a fishing rod casting a lure ahead. I walked non-stop for over four hours, feeling fit and active and in some way hypnotised by the forest, by the endless grandeur. Eventually, feeling hungry, I stopped by the creek with a view upstream to misty mountains. A heron flapped by and there were dippers in the water. It was a lovely spot and the rain had stopped. I had a lunch – I could hardly call it a late breakfast – of trail mix and creek water. I needed no more.

During the second half of the day the rain started again. Two parties of rather wet dishevelled backpackers came down the trail. I probably looked much the same. I camped at Beaver Pass campsite, for which I had a permit for two days earlier. After I was settled into the tent two others arrived. Rain woke me a few times during the night but it was dry at dawn. The two other campers were heating water over a small fire. Talking to them I discovered one was a guide and a writer who'd worked in the Pyrenees and climbed Ben Nevis. He was delighted I'd enjoyed the Kettle River Range as he was particularly fond of that area and involved in the campaign to protect it. He gave me his card. Craig Romano Writer it said. Amongst many other books he was author of the *Columbia Highlands* book about the Kettle River Range that I would read after the walk.

The campsite was a basic one, just some bare patches in the woods and a few fire rings. There was a pit toilet out of sight in the trees but no kitchen areas, bear poles, site maps or pitching platforms as there had been in Glacier National Park. The whole feeling was much more natural and wild without the feeling of over-control and organisation I'd felt in Glacier. In fact it was little different to many of the sites I'd used in the Pasayten Wilderness. The trails in the North Cascades were less groomed too and the carved wooden trail signs less intrusive than the more formal metal ones in Glacier. Overall I much preferred the ambience of the North Cascades National Park.

The day took me down to Little Beaver Creek and then along its eponymous trail to an ascent to 5206 foot/1587 metre Whatcom Pass, the high point of the PNT in the North Cascades National

Mount Baker, North Cascades

Park, and a descent along the Brush Creek Trail to the Chilliwack River valley. It was another day of big trees, clouds, rain and glimpses of the glories of the mountains. The Little Beaver Creek Valley was dramatic with high waterfalls pouring down cliffs from high barely visible glaciers. The climb to Whatcom pass was steep and I was impressed with the carefully engineered switchbacks that were in the process of reconstruction. The Chilliwack River was crossed by a high cable car, operated by pulling on the ropes, that was fun to use and gave unusual views up and down the river. I camped deep in the woods at the Copper Creek Campsite, another soggy camp with water dripping from the trees but also another basic site that felt simple and natural. Mary Janes Farm Organic Ginger Sesame Pasta made for a tasty and warming dinner. After ten days my sojourn in the wilderness was coming to an end. The next day I would leave the national park and join roads leading to the Mount Baker Ski Area. There was still another week's walking to the next town and I would still be in the Cascades but unspoilt wilderness and trail walking would now be broken by logged forests and roads.

On another cloudy, rainy day I followed the trail out of the national park and up to 5066 foot/1544 metre Hannegan Pass. High above through the swirling clouds I could just see glaciers on Ruth Mountain, which towers above the pass. Then it was down the Ruth Creek Trail to a trailhead with a PNT sign and a large car park. I met many parties ascending the trail including some climbers equipped with ropes and ice climbing gear, one wearing his helmet. A group of six day hikers quizzed me on my walk once they heard my accent as they were ex-pat Brits living in Vancouver. At the trailhead four young American hikers also showed an interest in the PNT and were very keen to give me some food in support of my walk. I accepted an apple.

A quiet gravel road continued along beside

Camp in the Mount Baker National Recreation Area with Mount Baker on the horizon

Ruth Creek. The rain stopped and there were touches of sunshine, which felt wonderful on my face, though mostly I was in shaded forest. Then I arrived at the paved road to the Mount Baker Ski Resort, 8 miles/13 kilometres of steep, winding and busy highway that I had to climb. There was little or no shoulder and the road was narrow in places with many tight bends. Some motorcyclists were using it as a race track and roared past me just inches away. Some of the cars were too fast and too close as well. Each time a vehicle missed me I breathed out with relief. I edged round each bend with trepidation. I'd felt safe in the wilderness. I felt in great danger here. Near the top of the road I had views of the massive glacier-clad north-west face of Mount Shuksan. This is a famous mountain as the sunlit view of it under a blue sky reflected in Picture Lake has appeared on everything from magazine covers to calendars, postcards and chocolate boxes. As I walked past Picture Lake was grey and rippled by the wind while clouds drifted across the face of the mountain, the scene bleached of colour. I guessed that Shuksan more often looked like this than it did in the well-known colourful images. In my journal I noted that 'photos might be best monochrome'. As I gazed at the mountain a car stopped, the driver asking what mountain it was, thinking it

might be Baker.

I plodded on up to the closed ski area, which felt desolate, strange and dead, though there were a few cars around and lights in some of the cabins. The silent, still lifts hung uselessly in the wind. I don't like downhill resorts much at any time but at least in winter with snow I can see their attraction. Outside of the ski season I find them ugly and dispiriting. Mount Baker Ski Area is famous for both the world's greatest recorded snowfall in one season – a phenomenal 95 feet/30 metres in 1998 – and the highest annual average snowfall, an equally astounding 53.4 feet/16.3 metres. This was hard to imagine as I looked at the grubby patches of snow that were all that remained of the last winter's snowfall.

10781 foot/3286 metre Mount Baker itself is a massive strato-volcano (a tall, steep, conical volcano – the classic shape in fact), one of the long line of such volcanoes that stretches north from Lassen Peak in Northern California and is part of the 'ring of fire' round the edge of the Pacific Ocean. I had hiked past many of these volcanoes on the Pacific Crest Trail, crossing the slopes of some, but had only seen Mount Baker as a distant white dome. Now I was crossing its flanks. Baker is reckoned the second most active of these volcanoes after Mount

St Helens and there were several small eruptions during the nineteenth century and some signs of activity in 1975. It's also the most glaciated, having more snow and ice than all the other volcanoes together other than Mount Rainier. There are thirteen glaciers in total, covering more than sixteen square miles/41 square kilometres. On the map Mount Baker forms a big ragged ring of white with only a few tiny brown patches signifying ice free ridges and rock outcrops. Native people called the mountain Kulshan. The European name Baker was given to it in 1792 by British explorer Captain George Vancouver during his famous expedition along the Pacific coast in honour of his third lieutenant Joseph Baker who made observations of it from onboard ship. The first recorded ascent of the mountain was in 1868 when it was climbed by a party of five led by mountaineer Edmund Coleman who had made two previous attempts. Today the easier ascent routes are regarded as straightforward and not technically difficult. Being on the western edge of the North Cascades, Mount Baker stands out in views from long distances away. From the ski area I would traverse its lower slopes on both the eastern and southern sides. Maybe if the weather cleared I might even see it. Most of Mount Baker is protected in the Mount Baker Wilderness Area.

However the PNT only runs through a small section of this and spends rather too much time on roads.

I descended into the Wilderness Area from the ski resort on the Lake Ann Trail, which ran down beside the East Fork of Swift Creek. It was dusk when I passed a sign announcing the wilderness. Rain was pounding down and the trail was wet and muddy and rooty and rocky. It was a trail though, a relief after the road. I sloshed through the creek twice as I hiked down it, flashing my headlamp either side in search of an area that wasn't too sodden or too sloping for a camp. Eventually I found a small bare area right next to the trail. It would have to do. Early in the night I was woken by flashlights and tramping feet as someone went down the trail. I was not the only hiker out in the rain and the dark. Much later it was heavy rain hammering on the tent that roused me. At dawn it was still raining and there were many puddles around the tent, one of them starting to run under the groundsheet. This had been the wettest night yet, and the rain was not over.

That night I was down in the valley on the roadside Boulder Creek Campground. It had been raining non-stop for 26 hours. Everything was damp and condensation was forming on the mesh walls of the inner tent and the ground round the tent was becoming waterlogged. I was just relieved to be there after one of the most difficult and dangerous and extraordinarily wet days of the walk. Splashing through the mud of the Swift Creek Trail from my camp I had been worried. Ahead lay a ford of the creek. On the map Li had written 'no bridge, water can be high'. In the guidebook Ron wrote 'the water will be too deep and fast to ford' and recommended finding a fallen tree to use as a bridge. Masses of white water cascades and streams were pouring down the steep hillsides and into Swift Creek, which was a tumbling torrent of seething, foaming water.

I reached the point where the trail crossed the creek. Here it was wide and fast and grey in colour. I could not see how deep it was. A cable had been slung across the creek as if for a cable car or pulley but there was no way to use it. I prospected downstream in search of fallen logs or gentler water, which involved desperate bushwhacking in the dense tangle of vegetation on the steep banks but produced nowhere to cross. I considered retreating back up to the ski area, which would have been sensible but which would have left me with a very long road walk round the northern side of Mount Baker that would take several days. Then I remembered seeing the creek split round a rock islet not far above the crossing place.

I thrashed through the bush to find water that looked a little less savage, a little less powerful. I ventured in and felt the water tugging me over. I backed off and tried again a few yards upstream. Again it felt too strong and I retreated. A third attempt and I felt more secure. Facing upstream and clinging to my poles I edged across. The water was crotch-deep and very strong. Half-way across I decided this was a mistake but also that going on would be easier than going back. I didn't want to stop or try and change direction. Eventually I made it to the far bank, shaking and tense but glad to be alive. If I'd known what it would be like I wouldn't have attempted it but now I was across I was pleased. To take my mind off the ford and what might have happened there followed an awful bushwhack back to the trail across a steep slope of springy alder, vine maple, prickly irritating devil's club, stinging nettles, spiky brambles and tough ferns. From reaching the crossing point to rejoining the trail on the far side had taken three and a half hours.

I hurried down the trail, knowing that not far ahead was Rainbow Creek, which I might also have to ford. On Li's map it said 'logs and cables across creek'. I was relieved to find they were still there. Log walking just above a raging, roaring torrent

might have been unnerving but after Swift Creek it felt easy and safe. Once over I could return to simple hiking.

Soon I left the wilderness area and had a decision to make. The official PNT made a big eastwards loop round Baker Lake. An alternative route stayed high above the west shore and cut out most of the distance. '8.5 ml vs. ~35 ml? You decide…' Li had written on the map. The clouds were brushing the tops of the forest. The rain was still pouring down. There seemed no reason to do the extra distance. In sunshine I would probably have done so. In this weather I was happy to take the shortest route, which led along forest roads past great, shaggy, moss-covered maples to another raging torrent, this one called Boulder Creek. There was a stout vehicle bridge across it however and a campground on the far side. I was down at 1,000 feet/300 metres here and yet still in the mist. I'd now had eight days and nine nights of mostly rain and high humidity. Everything was damp. I wrote in my journal 'should be just about comfortable tonight but I do need to dry and air stuff'.

The day felt strange when I woke. The rain had stopped. Mist still hung in the tree tops and the sky was overcast but it was a dry morning. I had another route decision to make not long after

Airing damp gear at the camp below Mount Baker

setting out. The choice was between the old route, as described in the original guidebook, which was all on roads or the new, 18 mile/29 kilometre longer route, marked on my maps, which involved some trails and climbed up into the Mount Baker National Recreation Area right at the foot of the glaciers on the south side of the mountain. Again I would let the weather decide. Low cloud and rain, low route. Clearing skies, high route. The first 3.5 miles/5.5 kilometres were on a paved road. I wore sandals so my feet were dry for the first time in well over a week. I passed some workmen repairing the road who told me the forecast was for good weather for the next four days. Given that and

Below Mount Baker, North Cascades

because it wasn't raining and I was already fed up with paved roads I took the longer, higher route, climbing up dirt roads through the forest to the

National Recreation Area (these are protected areas but without the regulations of wilderness areas – in this case snowmobiles are allowed, which they aren't in a designated wilderness). A trail now led up towards timberline and Mount Baker. As I climbed the clouds began to dissipate and the great white mountain was revealed; a tremendous vista of snow, glacier and rock. That afternoon and evening were the scenic highlight of the whole walk and all the more powerful and precious because of the days of cloud and rain that preceded them. Awestruck by the mighty mountain I took a sidetrip up the Railroad Grade, a narrow arête atop a moraine from which I looked directly across a glacier-fed creek to the heavily crevassed Easton Glacier and the summit of Mount Baker. The views were fantastic and the evening light beautiful. Back on the trail I wandered a short distance to camp in an open meadow with a view of Mount Baker rising above the forest and, to the west, the long jagged ridge of Twin Sisters Mountain, the westernmost high peak of the North Cascades. This was the finest camp site of the walk. I watched a fine sunset on the edge of Twin Sisters Mountain, then night came with a brilliant starry sky and a crescent moon. It was the eve of my birthday and I was deliriously happy.

The morning was perfect. The sky was clear and blue. I watched the first pink light touch the summit snows of Mount Baker. Soon the whole mountain was shining though I was still in the shade. Surprisingly there hadn't been a frost, the temperature only falling to 3.6°C/38.5°F. The morning light was lovely and I was in no hurry to leave. I needed to think practically as well as emotionally though so when the sun reached me I spread out all my gear on bushes and tree branches before returning to watching and photographing Mount Baker. Eventually, reluctantly, I packed up and departed. At first, on the trail to Bell Pass, there were enticing views of Mount Baker, with its satellite summits, Colfax Peak and Seward Peak, becoming more prominent, along with Twin Sisters Mountain. Then I rounded a corner to the pass and Baker disappeared and the day collapsed into the mundane. The rest of the day felt like a leaving of the North Cascades as I descended to the South Fork Nooksack River valley and then followed this down through the forest. The creek was pleasant and it was nice to sit in the sun beside it for a snack. I hadn't been able to do that for a while. The trail was quite rough in places, requiring concentration as it disappeared in tangles of vegetation. At one point it was washed away completely and I had

to cast around for a while before I found it some distance away from the creek. The wash-out was crossed on another log bridge with cable hand rail. Then the trail became a closed road with a series of humps and trenches, put in to stop vehicles using it. Climbing in and out of these disrupted the rhythm I expected when walking on roads. The closed road led to an open dirt road with recent tyre tracks and my rhythm returned as I followed it through logged forest before camping next to it. I'd gone from the superlative to the functional. I could see logging machinery on the hillside above the camp. Immediately around me was new growth around 10 feet/3 metres high. This type of country would be the norm from here to Puget Sound, about 70 miles/112 kilometres mostly on logging roads in logged forest. I wasn't looking forward to it but the glory of Mount Baker would inspire me and carry me onwards for many days.

Immediately I wanted to reach the city of Sedro Woolley in the next two or three days. Otherwise I would run out of food. Once I reached the highway into the town I intended hitch-hiking. The distance to the highway was around 40 miles/65 kilometres. In my journal I wrote 'mostly roads, little to see, no excuse not to march on'. That night the sky was again starry and I felt the place

was much improved in the dark. The logging scars were hidden and all I could see were just the edges of the trees against the sky. Soon after dawn I could hear machinery and horns as the logging operation began, which encouraged me to pack up and move on. This, I realised, was much easier and quicker in dry weather with dry gear. However after less than 48 hours of dryness the rain returned with a huge thunderstorm and a torrential downpour. Before the storm I'd had good views of Mount Baker rising white and proud above the ugly clear-cuts along the South Fork Nooksack River and climbed 3957 foot/1206 metre Mount Josephine, the lowest peak I'd ascended, via the East Ridge Trail. This provided some respite from the road walking with the narrow, steep east ridge even involving some easy rock scrambling amongst the dense, tangled forest. The rough trail was overgrown in places and in need of maintenance but it was exciting and involving compared with the road walking. The summit gave views back east to the now sunny Cascades and down to the cloudier wide Skagit Valley where there were highways and towns. After Josephine the rain came and it was back on logging roads to the slopes of Lyman Hill. I was in private forestry now and probably shouldn't have camped but I reckoned I'd be away in the morning

before anyone was likely to find me. It was another roadside camp, near a creek so I didn't have to carry water. The road to Sedro Woolley was just 18 miles/30 kilometres away. That evening I ate two of the MaryJanesFarm meals – Chili Mac and Bare Burrito. These organic meals were the tastiest trail dinners I had on the trip but the portions were quite small. I needed two. This explained the extra dinners in my supply box at Ross Lake Resort. Torrential rain woke me at midnight. Then I was awake a few more times as my airbed was leaking again. As soon it was flat I woke up as the ground under me was very stony.

A forgettable day of logging roads and rough trails led through clear-cuts and second growth forest across Lyman Hill and down to the Samish River valley, the little settlement of Wickersham and Highway 9. A coyote watching me was the only interesting point of the day. I read when I could, in between the showers. From Wickersham, where there were no facilities, the route led along the highway for nearly 3 miles/5 kilometres to the start of the next logged forest hill, Anderson Mountain. The road had narrow shoulders and the traffic was fast. It was a dangerous walk. I hoped I wouldn't have to hike the whole distance to Sedro Woolley. In fact, conveniently I was just past the turn-off

for Anderson Mountain when a truck stopped. The driver was a young friendly logger who took me to a motel in Sedro Woolley and who enthused about a backpacking trip he had taken to Mount Baker, saying he loved the outdoors.

With a population of over 10,000 Sedro Woolley was the largest town so far on the walk and a big shock after 18 days in the wilds. I was to become used to urban settings in the next week. I was now in the most populous section of the PNT. The Three Rivers Motel was fine and located within walking distance of the city centre, which was a relief. I rang Kris, who had said she would drive out and meet me here. Issaquah was just 68 miles/110 kilometres to the south. The next day, which I was taking off from the trail, she turned up with the last maps for the walk plus my box, which I'd mailed her from Oroville. Meeting her felt unreal, almost as if the walk was over, though I knew I still had around 250 miles/400 kilometres to walk. I felt generally disconnected anyway, wandering around in a dreamlike state and feeling like an observer in an alien world. Sedro Woolley was just too big. I did the usual chores automatically, my mind elsewhere. I patched the airbed again, which was hardly any easier in a warm room than it had been in the cold waters of Frosty Lake, and arranged to borrow one

Twin Sisters Mountain from the descent from the Mount Baker National Recreation Area

from Kris if it failed again.

I ate in restaurants of course but, oddly, I didn't have the pleasure in this break from dried trail food that I expected. There was nothing wrong with any of the meals but somehow they weren't memorable. I wasn't feeling connected enough with reality to really enjoy them. My one prize from

Sedro Woolley was a copy of the *National Audubon Society Field Guide to the Pacific Northwest*, a fairly weighty volume but one I would carry the rest of the way. Sitting in the bland motel room I identified some of the plants and animals I had seen from its pages.

CHAPTER 6

LOWLANDS AND ISLANDS

SEDRO WOOLLEY TO PORT TOWNSEND

September 18 – 22

91 miles/146 km

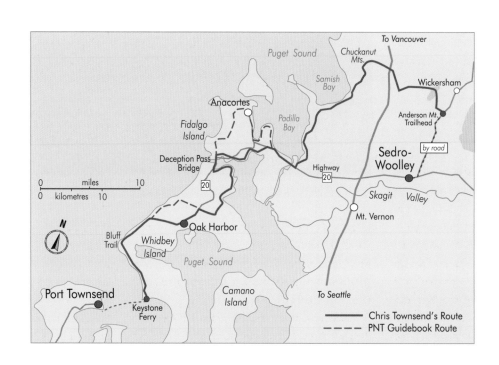

To Vancouver

Puget Sound

Chuckanut
Mts.

Wickersham

Samish
Bay

Anacortes

Padilla
Bay

Anderson Mt.
Trailhead

Fidalgo
Island

by road

Deception Pass
Bridge

Highway

Sedro-
Woolley

20

Skagit   Valley

0   miles   10

0   kilometres   10

Mt. Vernon

N

Bluff
Trail

Oak Harbor

Whidbey
Island

Puget Sound

Port Townsend

Keystone
Ferry

Camano
Island

To Seattle

—— Chris Townsend's Route
- - - PNT Guidebook Route

Back at the Anderson Mountain trailhead, courtesy of a $20 taxi ride from Sedro Woolley, I set out on my last day in the tail end of the Cascades, the line of low wooded hills that stretches out from Mount Baker to Puget Sound. The day was cloudy with showers that, as evening drew on, turned to steady rain. The walking over Anderson Mountain was on the now usual mix of trails and forest roads through clear-cuts and second growth trees, some of them quite big. The walking in the former was unpleasant, in the latter quite pleasant. There were hazy views west to sea and islands. I would soon reach the coast. After Anderson Mountain came Little Baldy and then the wonderfully named Chuckanut Mountains ('chuckanut' is a Native American word meaning, depending on which source is consulted 'beach on a bay with a small entrance' or 'long beach far from a narrow entrance' – which are clearly versions of the same phrase and refer to the coast along Puget Sound, which has a narrow entrance). I found it hard to distinguish between these rounded hills and felt distinctly uninspired. Maybe in fine weather I'd have gained more enjoyment from the day and been energised by good views of islands and mountains. As it was, another day in this damaged country just felt like a chore. I'd started late in the morning and I finished

Puget Sound from the descent from the Chuckanut Mountains

at midnight, when I arrived at Lizard Lake, high in the Chuckanuts, and pitched my tent in the dark on sodden ground amongst dripping trees. I was surprised to see two other tents pitched near the reed-rimmed pool.

Heavy rain and mist accompanied me again the next day as I descended down a series of trails to the coast, finally leaving the Cascade Mountains after 20 days. Again there were hazy views out through the clouds to the sea. At the base of the last trail was a big stone PNT marker. 883 miles to the Rocky Mountains, it read, and 223 to the Pacific Ocean. Soon afterwards I reached salt water. I felt a small sense of achievement and a subdued

feeling I should celebrate but these emotions were rather suppressed by the rain and the knowledge that I was leaving wild country for a while.

I now had five days of lowland walking ahead, mostly on roads but with some trails in a few places. This was the most unusual part of the PNT as it was away from the mountains and in a fairly heavily populated area. I would eat in many restaurants and walk through towns and villages and past houses and farms. The landscape and environment were very different to anywhere else on the walk. This was mostly managed land. Crossing this area was the only way to link the Cascades with the last mountain range on the route, the Olympics. There is no possible wilderness link, all the land in between being developed. The PNT also has to find a way down the coast of the great complex inlet of the ocean called Puget Sound and then cross this to the Olympic Peninsula.

Whilst I would not choose this area for long distance walking there were some attractive areas and plenty of bird life and seascapes. The history and geography of the area is interesting too. Take the trail off the high speed highways it follows in places, as is planned, and it would be safer. Take it off the minor roads and it would be more enjoyable as well. As it is, I felt there was too much road

Rain in the Chuckanuts

walking between the more scenic and interesting places and too few sections of trail. Many of the quiet back roads would make good cycle routes but were a little lacking in interest for walkers.

When you don't have to think about the terrain or navigation but are just walking along a paved road uninteresting surroundings quickly lead to boredom, at least for me. I read much of the time, at least when it wasn't raining.

However, as with the logged forests, I already knew and accepted that, as on almost any long distance walk, there would be less interesting sections that were walked mainly to maintain the continuity. As the latter was important to me I was resigned to coping with them and at no time did I consider skipping anywhere though I did sometimes long for a section to be over, particularly when hiking busy highways. I can't think of any walking less enjoyable or more dangerous than along the narrow edge of a road with heavy traffic roaring past inches away.

The route in this area is an intricate one that weaves a way down the east side of Puget Sound and then across Fidalgo and Whidbey Islands to the Keystone ferry that crosses the sea to Port Townsend on the north-east corner of the Olympic Peninsula. I began my urban-rural-coastal walk along Chuckanut Drive below the Chuckanut Mountains. Out over the grey rain-splashed sea I could see misty islands. I was more interested, though, in the first restaurant along the road,

Chuckanut Manor, as it offered an opportunity to escape the still teeming rain and have a meal somewhere warm and dry as a celebration for reaching the coast. It was a good decision as the food was excellent and, having quizzed me about the walk as dripping hikers with big packs were obviously not usual customers, the owner offered me a free dessert. I felt I deserved it.

Back in the rain I followed roads along the shore of Samish Bay and then across marshy fields to Padilla Bay, a National Estuarine Research Reserve, its mudflats and tidal areas protected from development. The bay is in the delta of the Skagit River and because of sediment deposited by the latter it is very shallow and mostly uncovered at low tide. This makes it a suitable habitat for eelgrass, on which much wildlife depends, including commercially harvested sea creatures like salmon, crab and herring. There are over 8000 aces of eelgrass meadows in Padilla Bay.

I finished the day at the Bay View State Park campground, set on the edge of the water. I walked the last section in the dark, on long flat roads with the thin line of orange lights of the city of Anacortes on Fidalgo Island glowing across the water. Earlier I had watched herons fishing in mudflat creeks, red-tailed hawks floating overhead

and an owl perched on a telephone wire. There wasn't much traffic. One driver stopped to offer a lift. A cyclist passed me then turned back and came alongside, curious as to where I was hiking. He had finished the Appalachian Trail in the Eastern USA just a month earlier.

My second lowland day was a mix of trails, quiet back roads and the horrendous State Highway 20, a road I came to hate. The Padilla Bay Trail made for a pleasant start, despite the steady rain, as it wound through mudflats and across slow winding creeks. There were many herons. Ahead, though, I could see hell in the form of heavy traffic. Highway 20 was a very busy high speed road along

Pacific Northwest Trail marker in the Chuckanut Mountains

which I trudged for an hour, feeling battered by the roar of the traffic, terrified by the speed and somewhat sickened by the smell. The forests and mountains seemed far away. The highway took me across the high curving Swinomish Channel Bridge, which apparently gives good views in fine weather, onto Fidalgo Island where I was able to escape the thundering vehicles for quieter roads along which I found the Trestle coffee shop, another refuge from the rain, which had excellent paninis and coffee and the fastest wi-fi of anywhere on the walk. The café is also a social venture with profits going to support orphan children in Africa and other parts of the world. Fidalgo Island is named after Spanish explorer Salvador Fidalgo who explored the area in 1790, though he didn't realise that it was an island, separated from the mainland by the narrow Swinomish Channel. Its island identity wasn't discovered until 1841, when American naval officer Charles Wilkes explored Puget Sound.

The Trestle coffee shop is named for the old railway trestle that crosses Fidalgo Bay to Anacortes. The trestle has been converted into a hiker/cyclist bridge and runs for almost a mile/1.5 kilometres. It looks a scenic route but unfortunately had been damaged by fire the year before. I had been told it was still closed (in fact the repaired trestle had

reopened a few months earlier) so I needed a different route. The alternative way to Anacortes involved two miles/3 kilometres on the highway. I wanted to avoid busy roads whenever possible and I didn't want to walk through any more towns than necessary anyway, though I would have hiked the trestle route for its own sake if I'd known it was open, so I took another alternative route described in the guidebook that avoided Anacortes and went instead to pleasant, quiet Similk Beach and then across Fidalgo Island south of the town. To reach this route I first had to cross Highway 20. Signs said pedestrians were not allowed to cross. I ignored them and managed to dodge the traffic. It was probably no more dangerous than the ford of Swift Creek. A low narrow neck of land separates Fidalgo Bay from Similk Beach. As Ron says in the guidebook it would only take a slight rise in sea level for the two to connect, making Fidalgo two islands. As the climate warms I would think this is quite likely in the not too distant future.

Beyond Similk Bay I had to risk my life along Highway 20 again, though only for a short distance. Mostly I was on quiet roads across the island to the west side where I was pleased to find the new Pass Lake Trail, which led through quiet and attractive woodland to Deception Pass Bridge, which links

Pacific Northwest Trail signs, Deception Pass State Park

Fidalgo and Whidbey Islands. I reached Deception Pass late in the afternoon just as the sun emerged below the clouds to cast a lovely soft golden light

Deception Pass Bridge between Whidbey and Fidalgo Islands.

and now a National Historic Monument, I followed a trail through the woods and over Goose Rock hoping to find somewhere quiet and with water to camp. Goose Rock was a nice, wild, glacier-scraped little rock but I failed to find a campsite or water so descended back to Highway 20 and the big Deception Pass State Park Cranberry Campground, set in some fine old growth cedar forest. The next morning I wandered down to big Cranberry Lake and sat watching the reflections of clouds in the water, a peaceful scene. Although very close to the beach and barely above sea level this is a freshwater lake.

Whidbey Island is a long, thin island – roughly 35 miles/56 kilometres long by 1.5 to 12 miles/2.4 to 19 kilometres wide-with a convoluted coastline. Nearly 60,000 people live on the island, with tourism, farming and a Naval Air Station the biggest employers. For the walker Whidbey has some good trails and much bird and sea life. The PNT runs the length of the island.

From the Cranberry Campground the route followed roads and trails, some in impressive forest, round the east side of Whidbey Island to big Dugualla Bay where there were many birds – tall, thin-legged herons standing solitary staring into the water, strange prehistoric-looking cormorants

on the sea, the woods and the bridge. Deception Pass is so called because George Vancouver, who explored the area in 1792, at first thought Whidbey Island was a peninsula. Eventually his head navigator, Joseph Whidbey, showed that it was actually a sea channel connecting the Strait of Juan de Fuca to the west with Skagit Bay and Puget Sound to the east. Feeling the topography had deceived them Vancouver gave the channel its name. Joseph Whidbey also circumnavigated the island, after which Vancouver named it for him.

Highway 20 runs over Deception Pass Bridge but for once there is a safe walkway for hikers. Once across the attractive iron bridge, built in 1935

Sunset over Puget Sound from Deception Pass Bridge

perched on posts with their wings spread, flocks of black and white Canada geese floating on the sea and masses of white gulls in the air and on the water. Curiosities were a jumble of old faded and battered picnic tables at the end of a forest road and a tsunami warning sign, the latter a reminder of the ring of fire and the danger of earthquakes and volcanic activity along the Pacific coast. As the day wore on the sun came out. There had been no rain for the first time in a week. The road walking ended in the city of Oak Harbor, where I checked into the Queen Ann Motel. Here I was asked for I.D. by the owner, who looked and sounded Indian (Asian Indian that is, not American Native). I produced my passport and was told it wouldn't do, I had to have an identity card, which everyone had to carry in the USA (not so, in fact). Eventually I persuaded her that my passport really did confirm my identity and, although still evidently suspicious, she let me stay. No one else on the trip ever asked me for identity apart from the Border Guards and even they didn't query the validity of my passport.

Oak Harbor is a sizeable town, the largest on Whidbey Island, with a population of around 20,000. I most enjoyed the cafes and the evening light over the harbour itself with a full moon hanging in a blue sky that faded into pink and was reflected in the almost still sea, a lovely, peaceful, scene.

From Oak Harbor I headed back to the west side of the island and the best walking in the whole of this lowland section on the Bluff Trail, which runs along the steep, loose, sandy bluffs that rise above the beach. Mostly the trail wove a way in and out of the forest on the top of the bluffs, which reach a height of 270 feet/82 metres, and which give excellent views out to sea and round the curving bluffs along the coast. At one point I descended the bluffs, a plunge down the steep sand on my heels that felt like descending a soft snow slope, to reach the beach, just a thin strip of pebbles and wet sand as the tide was high. Bleached logs lay on the beach, one of them a whole tree with its trunk buried in the sand and the branches curving into the air like the bones of a dinosaur skeleton. Across the sea I could see the dark outline of the Olympic Peninsula. Although I was in sunshine – a second day without rain – clouds hid the mountains. Down on the beach I passed the blue waters of Peregos Lagoon, formed by a spit of land. On the map the lagoon was shown as one body of water. When I passed by this had split into two. Not far beyond the lagoon I reached Ebay's Landing, named for one Colonel Isaac Neff Ebay who was one of the first white settlers on the island in the 1850s, coming here to farm the rich land. In 1857 however he was killed by local natives in revenge for the killing of one of their chiefs.

A final road walk led to the Keystone Ferry landing from where ferries cross the 5 miles/8 kilometres of Admiralty Inlet, which links the Strait of Juan de Fuca with Puget Sound, to Port Townsend. Admiralty Inlet is a major shipping lane, connecting the ports of Seattle and Tacoma with the Pacific Ocean. Taking the ferry did finally break the walk but this is the route of the PNT and the only way of walking the whole way would be a very long road slog round the end of Puget Sound that would take many days and reach the Olympic Peninsula far from the mountains. I wanted to be back in the wilds as soon as possible. Purists may well feel that a canoe or other boat should have been used. However, not being a canoeist, sailor, swimmer or any type of water person I had long ago accepted that if there was water that was too deep to wade across then I would walk to a bridge or take a ferry. I'd learnt this the hard way eighteen years before this walk when I'd spent a summer walking the length of Norway and Sweden. In arctic Sweden I'd followed the Kungsleden long distance path, which crosses a number of long lakes. Rowing

Cranberry Lake, Deception Pass State Park, Whidbey Island

boats are provided for hikers and locals also run ferries. I would row if I could, I thought. I came to the first big lake, Aktse, and climbed into the rowing boat sitting in the shallow water at the edge of a small bay. The water looked calm. It was 2 miles/3 kilometres to the far side. I rowed clumsily out into the main lake. The water wasn't calm. A strong wind was blowing down the lake, creating waves that pushed the boat sideways and rocked it alarmingly. I quickly found I couldn't row well or fast enough to defeat the waves and was going down the lake not across it. Somehow I managed to turn the boat round and make it back to a stony headland about 500 yards down the lake from where I'd begun. The thirty minutes in the boat were the most terrifying of that walk. The next day I happily paid the 50 kroner for the little open ferry that appeared early in the morning. The phlegmatic ferryman looked knowingly at the rowing boat beached down the lake but said nothing. I did not attempt to row across any further lakes and knew that on future walks I wouldn't even consider crossing large bodies of water under my own steam. I would walk every yard on land but accept that lakes and seas were for people who knew what they were doing. Four years after the Scandinavian trek I did a long walk over all the 3,000 foot/914 metre summits in Scotland. One of those peaks lay on the island of Mull. I caught the ferry there and back and never considered any other options.

From the ferry I could see the warm red brick buildings of Port Townsend slowly growing larger under an evening sky dappled with pink clouds. This was my last town stop and I would spend a day here doing the usual chores for the final time. Happily, it was one of the finest stops on the walk; a lovely old town full of character with many well-preserved Victorian buildings and a friendly, artistic ambience. In the guidebook Ron agreed, calling the town 'quaint' (I think in praise) and saying that it was 'a "must" for PNT aficionados' and that hikers

Dugualla Bay, Whidbey Island

should 'plan to surrender to the town's spell and stay a while.' I fully intended to do just that.

I was pleased Port Townsend was so pleasant and interesting partly, of course, because it shared my name, though in fact it was originally named Port Townshend by, yet again, George Vancouver (an inescapable presence in the history of the whole Pacific Northwest coast) in 1792 for the Marquess Townshend, a British peer and a friend of his. Over time the 'h' was lost and a community grew up around this safe harbour, becoming incorporated as a city in 1851 when it was hoped it would become the major port in the area, to which end it was known as the 'City of Dreams'. This ambition came to nothing however, with Seattle becoming, and remaining, the dominant port, and Port Townsend becoming somewhat of a quiet backwater.

Wanting to fully absorb the atmosphere I booked into the old Waterstreet Hotel, built in 1889, right in the centre of town. The hotel had been renovated in traditional style and fitted in with the Victorian feel of Port Townsend and was a wonderful place to base myself. Entry to the hotel was through the Pacific Traditions Gallery, which had an interesting collection of Native American art, as the hotel was on the second and third floors of the building. Walking round the town the next

View from the Bluff Trail down the coast of Whidbey Island to the Peregos Lagoon

day I was also impressed with the amenities – bookstores, outdoor stores, an organic wholefood co-op – as well as the atmosphere. Viewing these along with many arts and crafts shops I wasn't surprised to read that Port Townsend was a 'hippy magnet' in the 1960s and that 'a lot of our "hippies" opened small shops downtown'. That

influence is still very evident and as a child of the sixties myself I liked it and felt at home. Everything was easy walking distance too, making this just about the perfect town for a day off from hiking. I collected my box for the last time and swapped my airbed, which I'd failed to repair successfully so it was still slowly deflating every night, for

one of Kris's that she'd put in the box. Talking to Kris on the phone she said she'd like to join me for the last few days along the Olympic coast and would rent a bear resistant container for me, as one was a requirement on that stretch, which is in the Olympic National Park, not because of bears but because of racoons, which climb well, making hanging food no defence. I also rang the Olympic National Park ranger service about permits for the national park and the very helpful ranger told me I could issue myself one at a trailhead, which was excellent news.

The library had computers and internet access so I spent a few hours there answering emails and writing my third report for TGO magazine. Denise seemed well and happy. I was looking forward to seeing her again. I felt I'd been away for a long time. Other emails were from editors asking for pieces for forthcoming articles and books. They knew I would be home before too long. Replying to say yes, I could do the work, brought home to me that the adventure was nearing its end. I was determined to enjoy the last days.

Courtesy of a Facebook message I heard from my friend John Manning that Nacho, who he'd met on the Pacific Crest Trail in 2004, had finished on September 21, presumably with Pepper, the day

I had walked into Oak Harbor. Given that they'd passed me 15 days before that in the Cascades that meant they'd walked around 500 miles/800 kilometres in 15 days, about 33 miles/53 kilometres per day. I was averaging about half that. John did say that he'd been unable to keep up with Nacho on the PCT.

Amongst the restaurants and bars I discovered, the Sirens Pub, barely a step away from the hotel, had excellent food and a great selection of micro-brews for the evenings and the Silverwater Café was equally excellent for coffee and food during the day. The Food Co-op provided the best selection of trail food I had found anywhere on the PNT, all

Dusk, Oak Harbor, Whidbey Island

The "dinosaur" tree

organic. I would eat well during the last section of the walk. In The Imprint Bookstore I found another book by Jack Nisbet, whose interesting *Sources of the River* about David Thompson and the Columbia River I'd read earlier in the walk. This book was called *The Collector* and told the story of Scottish plant collector David Douglas, who had explored the Pacific Northwest in search of new plants in the 1820s and 30s and who had given his name to the Douglas fir. He'd also had a huge influence on the environment in Britain, sending back seeds of many plants that grew as well in the equally ocean-influenced cool wet climate of Britain as they did in the Pacific Northwest. One tree in particular, the Sitka spruce, was to become the dominant species for commercial plantations in Britain where it was packed into dense rows and harvested long before it reached maturity. In Scotland it is now by far the most common tree. Soon I was to see it in its native habitat and realise just what a magnificent tree it could be.

Enjoyable though Port Townsend was, after a day there I thought I ought to continue the walk. I was feeling somewhat detached from the trail though, something I hadn't experienced before. When I considered the last week I understood why. My second night in Port Townsend would be the

eighth since reaching Sedro Woolley. Five of those nights had been spent in accommodation in towns and of the three spent camping only one was a wild camp, the others being on organised roadside campgrounds. Then during the day there had been many roads, vehicles, buildings and people. I was losing touch with the wild, losing contact with the

reasons for the walk. I needed to head back into the mountains.

Port Townsend from the ferry from Whidbey Island

The beach, Whidbey Island

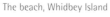

CHAPTER 7

BIG TREES, WILD OCEAN

Port Townsend to Cape Alava
September 24 - October 2
260 miles/418 km

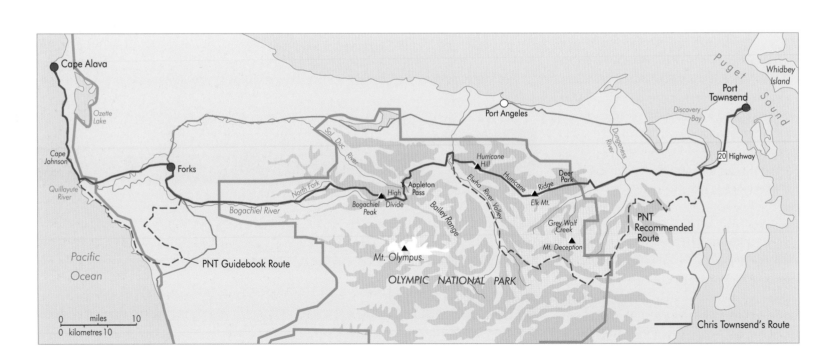

Cape Alava

Whidbey
Island

Ozette
Lake

Port
Townsend

Port Angeles

Discovery
Bay

Puget Sound

Cape
Johnson

Forks

20 Highway

Sol Duc River

Hurricane
Hill

Dungeness
River

Quillayute
River

North Fork

Appleton
Pass

High
Divide

Elwha River Valley

Hurricane
Ridge

Deer
Park

Bogachiel River

Bogachiel
Peak

Elk Mt.

PNT
Recommended
Route

Pacific
Ocean

Bailey Range

Grey Wolf
Creek

Mt. Deception

PNT Guidebook Route

Mt. Olympus.

OLYMPIC   NATIONAL   PARK

0   miles   10
0 kilometres 10

Chris Townsend's Route

The Olympic Peninsula is home to a temperate rain forest, the glacier-clad Olympic Mountains and a wild Pacific coast. Much of it lies in the 853,000 acre Olympic National Park and 95% of the park is designated wilderness. There are also wilderness areas in the Olympic National Forest that surrounds the main part of the park, which consists of the Olympic Mountains. Separated from the mountain core by a band of private forestry is a coastal strip that is also part of the National Park. Protruding out into the Pacific Ocean the Olympic Peninsula has a wet climate. 12 to 14 feet/3.5-4.5 metres of rain a year falls in the rain forests on the western side of the peninsula, the wettest place in the 48 contiguous states. I was not expecting this last section of the walk to be dry. I was looking forward to it though, to being in high mountains again and to walk through the giant trees of the rain forest. I'd never visited the Olympics before so this would all be new country.

First I had to escape Port Townsend and its environs. The town sits on the Quimper Peninsula, a little protrusion in the north-east corner of the Olympic Peninsula. The mountains and the national park were a day or more away. I set off in rain with low cloud over the hills, which felt the normal state of affairs now. The way out of town led from the

Mist in the Olympic Mountains along Hurricane Ridge, Olympic National Park

old historic area to the marina and wharf where an old railway line has been turned into a trail. I followed this past the big paper mill on the edge of town and into mixed farmland and woodland where trails and bits of road led to a cross-roads called Four Corners on the edge of big Discovery Bay. Here I joined the dreaded Highway 20 yet

again. It had sneaked over on the ferry with me in the guise of State Route 20. It wasn't as busy here but there was virtually no shoulder to walk on and the traffic was fast. For the first and only time in the guidebook Ron advised against hiking a section of the PNT and in no uncertain terms – 'do not try it!' 'End-to-enders', he continues 'are

hereby granted absolution to take the bus'. I had no intention of doing so. If I could walk I would. The distance on the highway was about 6 miles/9.5 kilometres. Although heavy lorries screaming past inches away were as terrifying as ever this section of Highway 20 was no more hazardous than the sections I'd already hiked. Overall I reckoned the hours I spent walking this main road constituted the most dangerous parts of the walk. Wilderness hazards – falling off a cliff, a bear attack, drowning, hypothermia, being struck by lightning – were all highly unlikely and not even a consideration most of the time. Being hit by a vehicle while walking along a road seemed much more likely. Perhaps Ron was right. Hikers should stick to the safety of the wilderness. The plan is for the PNT to follow a pipeline cut in the forest to the east of the highway on the Quimper Peninsula. When that section opens life will be much safer for PNT hikers.

With great relief I left the highway at the foot of Discovery Bay for a tangle of logging roads in various states of repair, some of them looking regularly used, some overgrown, some almost faded from existence. Much of the land was private and fenced off, occasionally with fields and livestock, including some imperious-looking llamas that peered curiously at me. Amongst the usual

'Keep Out' and 'Posted Private' notices were some stranger ones. 'No Peeing', said one in big letters, on the edge of a field in which I think cattle regularly ignored this command. Another made it very clear that visitors were very unwelcome – 'No Poachin' No Trespassin' NO NUTHIN'. This applies to friends, relatives, enemies and YOU. VIOLATERS WILL BE PROSECUTED'. Just in case the message hadn't got through the word 'violaters' had been crossed out and 'survivors' written underneath. I plodded on into the Olympic National Forest, where I needn't worry about inadvertently urinating on someone's piece of ground. Safe on public land I soon stopped to camp on some bare ground next to a dirt road.

The Needles and Mount Deception from the Obstruction Point Trail on Hurricane Ridge

The Obstruction Peak Trail, Olympic National Park

The Obstruction Point Trail on Hurricane Ridge

It was another functional forest camp but it was at least semi-wild. The weather had improved too with the rain stopping and some late sunshine bringing a touch of warmth and colour. After sunset long streaks of pink cloud lined up in the sky, a fine display. The forecast was mixed with sunshine, rain and cloud all predicted for the next few days. I just hoped I would see the mountains at some point.

The next day took me over the 1000 mile/1600 kilometres mark and back into the mountains. The weather was clear and sunny too, with enticing views of the hills to come. Yet it was still a frustrating day, and a long one too. I woke to a tent soaked with dew and condensation; a nice change from rain. I could hear bird calls. A loud jay screeched from a tree above the tent. The ground was crawling with slugs – big black ones and several of the rather disturbing-looking black-spotted yellow ones called, unsurprisingly, banana slugs. The walking began uneventfully enough along the forest road, which soon gave way to a better quality gravel road beside fields and habitations in the Johnnycomelately Creek valley that in turn became a paved road. Soon enough I was back in the forest on gravel and then dirt roads and descending to the Dungeness River with good views up river to the mountains. I was excited. I would be on a trail soon and heading into the wilderness. Or so I thought. Then I reached the trailhead for the Gray Wolf River Trail and noticed a scrap of paper, a page torn from a notebook, in a plastic bag pinned to the Forest Service notice board. It was dated the 9th September, sixteen days earlier, and read 'Attention: Trail 4½ miles ahead is dangerous and impassable'. The map showed the trail running along the narrow, steep-sided Gray Wolf valley. I could see a landslide or flood could easily wipe out the trail in there. The note was signed 'John N Calhoun PNT Thruhiker aka Mothernature's Son'. A card gave his outdoor experience – Appalachian Trail, Pacific Crest Trail, Colorado Trail, Yukon River,

International Appalachian Trail, Arizona Trail, Continental Divide Trail. This was clearly a man who knew what he was doing and I thought there was little point going to see for myself. I'd assume that if such an experienced wilderness traveller said it was impassable then it was. Mentally I thanked him for the courtesy of leaving the note and saving me, and probably others, nine extra miles/14 kilometres.

This left me with a dilemma, though, so I sat down to study the maps. Li marked the current official PNT route as making a big loop to the south and mostly staying in valleys. I wanted to take the original route, however, as described in Ron's guidebook as this involved a high level ridge walk that he described as one of the PNT's "Ten Best" and at its highest point as 'one of the few places anywhere on the PNT that is truly alpine'. Ron's description of Hurricane Ridge, as it was called, had been one of the places that had drawn me to the PNT in the first place. I didn't want to miss it. But how would I now reach the start? The maps showed only one option, a big loop to the north on logging roads that would bring me to the trail that led up to the start of the ridge, the same trail I'd hoped to reach via the Gray Wolf River Trail. I wanted Hurricane Ridge enough to go that way. It was a Saturday and there were quite a few vehicles

on the roads and a few people practising shooting in cleared areas beside the road. It was not a quiet walk and I didn't enjoy it. The rewards would come later. They began with the Deer Ridge Trail which led up into the national park and the wildest country since Mount Baker ten days previously. The climb was steep – 2900 feet/885 metres in

Black-tailed deer on Hurricane Ridge

5 miles/8 kilometres – and it was dusk when I set off. The evening was beautiful though with a clear sky, an orange moon, bright stars and the silhouettes of mountains. The trail ended at Deer Park at the start of Hurricane Ridge, a big campground accessible by road. It being a weekend it was packed with tents and vehicles. There are small 'walk-in' sites

for hikers though and these were free so I pitched my tent on one at the edge of the forest then walked through the campground to the creek at the start of Hurricane Ridge, the only water source. Returning to camp I noticed the sky was clouding over and the wind was picking up.

There followed an extremely wet night with constant heavy rain and a gusty wind. By dawn the hard-packed dirt of the site was sodden and for the first time a peg had pulled out of the ground, which explained why the rear of the tent was swaying in the wind. The rain cleared as it grew light however, leaving high clouds streaking overhead. With the logging roads diversion the previous day had been longer than planned, some 19 miles/30 kilometres that took me over 12 hours. This day would be even longer. Another route dilemma was coming up, this time one I had known about for some time. From Hurricane Ridge the PNT descended to the Elwha River valley where it was joined by the new southern route. Then the PNT runs along the Boulder Creek Trail to the Olympic Hot Springs, except that when I was there the first section of this trail was closed while work went on to remove two dams on the Elwha, freeing the river. The alternative route offered by the National Park was a 28 mile walk/45 kilometres, of which 15 miles/24 kilometres were on paved highway and much of which was outside the park. I really didn't want to break up my last wilderness sojourn with such a walk nor did I want to hike for hours on a highway. On the PNT route the distance was just 8 miles/13 kilometres. I had an idea of what I would do instead but decided to leave a decision until later. First I had Hurricane Ridge to enjoy. Before leaving I filled out a trail permit, guessing where I might be each night, and stuffed it in a pocket.

Just as Ron had said this was one of the highlights of the whole PNT, a spectacular mountain walk. From Deer Park the narrow, stony, Obstruction Point Trail traversed Green Mountain, Maiden Peak and Elk Mountain, initially in a timberline forest of small wind and cold stunted western white pine and subalpine fir and then open meadows gold and red with autumn colours and finally bare slopes of loose shale. There was a glorious feeling of being high above the world. I was back in the mountains. Inside I shouted with joy. This was what the walk was all about. To the south the deep valleys were swirling with cloud with high rock peaks and glaciers appearing and disappearing. On distant Gray Wolf Ridge I could see the ragged line of The Needles and steep 7788 foot/2374 metres) Mount Deception, a superb alpine vista. The trail climbs almost to the summit of 6779 foot/2066 metres Elk Mountain. Timberline is lower in the Olympics than in the other mountain ranges along the PNT so this is well above the trees, where in the Selkirks, say, it would be well in them. The feeling of being high in the mountains is all about the landscape and the terrain rather than the altitude and this felt truly alpine.

Unlike the other mountain ranges on the PNT, which are all parts of long south-north running chains, the Olympic Mountains make up a distinct unit separate from other ranges. The mountains form a very rough circle from which eleven main rivers radiate like the spokes of a wheel. Formed by the movement of tectonic plates that uplifted the land around 12 million years ago the Olympics are built of layers of sedimentary rock, mainly sandstone and shale, plus basalt, an igneous rock that came from undersea eruptions. In age the rocks run from 55 million to 15 million years old meaning that, like the Cascades, this is a geologically young mountain range. Also like the Cascades the current shape of the mountains has been formed by glaciation, which continues in a small way today, along with other erosion, to slowly wear down the mountains. The wet climate of the Olympic Peninsula means that much

Autumn colours on Hurricane Ridge

precipitation falls on the mountains, mostly as snow at high altitudes, so they have many glaciers and permanent snowfields. The mountains aren't high compared with the Cascades or the Rockies with Mount Olympus, the highest, reaching 7980 feet/2432 metres, but they are steep and rugged, a true alpine range.

The modern name of the Olympic Mountains was given them by a British explorer and fur trader in 1788. Captain John Meares was quite taken with them, saying they were so beautiful the gods could dwell there, so he called them 'Mount Olympus' after the home of the gods in Greece. It's hard to imagine Zeus or Aphrodite so far from their warm and dry Mediterranean home. The Norse gods, especially Thor, the god of storms, would seem more suitable. Previously the Olympics had been called "Sun-a-do" by the local Indians and, briefly, 'Sierra Nevada de Santa Rosalia' – the Snowy Mountains of Saint Rosalia – a name given by Spanish explorer Juan Perez in 1774. Meares name was the one that stuck and they became the Olympic Mountains and the land on which they stood the Olympic Peninsula. The first recorded ascent of Mount Olympus itself wasn't until 1907, when it was climbed by a party from The Mountaineers of Seattle, then a newly formed mountaineering club, now a leading

outdoor recreation and conservation organisation. Olympus is not an easy climb, being hard to reach, in an area of very high precipitation and technically quite difficult with a crevassed glacier to cross and some rock climbing. The shortest route involves 5,000 feet/1525 metres of ascent.

Staring out at the mountains in wonder I continued along the narrow trail as it curved across the steep slopes of Obstruction Peak to its terminus at Obstruction Point, still high on Hurricane Ridge at 6100 feet/1859 metres. Here it joined a gravel road that was originally intended, before the national park was created, to extend all the way to Deer Park. However the loose unstable slopes of Elk Mountain presented too big a problem for the road builders. Even though the second section of Hurricane Ridge is along this road it is still a fine walk with superlative views across the Elwha River valley to the line of high mountains known as the Bailey Range. As I contemplated this road walk over a snack and stared out over the dark forested valleys to the mountains a tame black-tailed deer approached me, clearly after food. I took its photograph but kept my snack. A nearby sign headed 'Backcountry Tactics' advised 'from this point on, meet the wilderness on its own terms' and warned of hypothermia and fast changes in the

weather, telling readers to bring layers of clothing, a good idea and one which I'd followed. On this day I was wearing a windshirt over my hiking shirt due to a cold breeze. The suggestion for a wool shirt and sweater and the pictures of a man in an old-fashioned looking check lumberjack shirt indicated that this was quite an old sign. It also said 'if you plan to cross any high passes, carry an ice ax and know how to use it', which advice was accompanied by a picture of someone showing how not to do a self-arrest with an ice axe – it would be ripped out of your hands held as shown – though I don't think that was the intention. Having got this far without an ice axe I sincerely hoped I wasn't going to need one. I understood the warning though. Hurricane Ridge receives 30-35 feet/9-10.5 metres of snow every year, much of which lasts into summer, and I'd just crossed slopes that could be avalanche prone and where an ice axe could be needed for security. This huge snow depth is one of the reasons for the many meadows along Hurricane Ridge as it prevents trees from growing in those areas.

From Obstruction Point the road wound along Hurricane Ridge, mostly below the crest, for some 9 miles/14 kilometres before it turned away to descend, leaving the PNT to continue along the ridge on a trail. The views were cloudier as I hiked

Sunset over the Olympic Mountains from the Hurricane Hill Trail

Log bridge, Olympic National Park

round, a coffee, a bun and some chocolate. Long distance hikers never pass by an opportunity to buy calories! Not far beyond the Visitor Centre I joined the Hurricane Hill Trail, which was initially paved but soon became a real wilderness trail. As I followed it across the open slopes of Hurricane Hill itself I watched in awe as a superb subtle sunset developed over glacier-clad 6995 foot/2132 metre Mount Carrie with the Elwha valley below now filled with thick white clouds. The scene was one of those that is so splendid, so unbelievably beautiful, that they make me shiver with delight. I lingered on the heights, watching the wonderful light constantly change and taking many photographs. Then as the light faded and the world began to turn grey I began descending into the cloud below.

The descent was a massive one, from 5600 feet/1707 metres to just 400 feet/122 metres, from the chilly, windswept heights into the warm depths of a densely forested valley. I was on open hillside at first where following the trail in the growing dark was fairly easy. Then I passed through the first trees and reached a steep meadow thick with vegetation, by which time it was dark. The trail switchbacked down this meadow, a darker line in the dark vegetation. I could just follow it though I had to watch carefully for the places where it suddenly

the road but still good. On reaching a National Park Visitor Centre that sits next to the road an hour before closing time I popped in for a quick look

turned back on itself. So far I hadn't switched on my headlamp though I had prudently removed it from my pack and put it in my shirt pocket. Beyond the meadow the trail entered a forest of huge Douglas firs. Suddenly I could see very little and I quickly tripped over the first invisible bump on the trail – a rock or a root – and conceded defeat. On went the headlamp and the world suddenly shrank to its circle of light. The huge trunks of the firs loomed up abruptly as I continued the descent, locked into the headlamp beam.

Finally I reached the valley floor. There was a road down here and a few buildings, some with lights on. All was quiet though. I knew there was a campground too but during the descent I had made my decision. I would hike the closed section of trail now, in the dark, late on a Sunday evening, which seemed an ideal time to do so without disturbing anyone or being disturbed. I walked quietly down the road past the campground to the closed section. There was a closed notice and a few barriers but these were easy to walk round. Below there were lights on the Upper Elwha Dam. I kept my headlamp switched off. It was 11 p.m.. The closed section was 6 miles/9.5 kilometres long, all of it on a dirt road that I could easily follow without need of a light. To aid me the clouds cleared and the

Clouds clearing from the High Divide peaks, Olympic National Park

Dusk from the Low Divide, Olympic National Park

moon came out, casting pale shadows. As the road made a rising traverse on the slopes above Lake Mills I could see many lights along the lakeshore. Once I turned away from the lake into the Boulder Creek valley they vanished though and I was alone with the forest and the night, the moon and the stars.

At the road end I was surprised to see a collection of big diggers and bulldozers. This was far from the dam removal site. The next surprise was the last two miles/3 kilometres to the Olympic Hot Springs where I intended to camp. The guidebook said the road from here on was closed to vehicles. It had been recently reopened and rebuilt though,

with a firm levelled surface and new bridges over every creek except for the last one, Crystal Creek, immediately before the Hot Springs. Here another bulldozer was parked. The trail down to the creek had been washed-out, a plank spanning the rushing waters at the bottom of the loose slopes. A short-climb out of the creek ravine and I reached the Boulder Creek Campground, 32 miles/52 kilometres and 16.5 hours since I had set out, making this the longest day by far in both distance and time. The campground was big and set amongst huge Douglas firs. Unsurprisingly, no-one else was there. Needing to eat before I slept I had a quick supper of a tortilla and a piece of cheese plus three-quarters of a bar of Green & Blacks organic ginger chocolate, bought for a treat, which I reckoned I now deserved, all washed down with a mug of hot chocolate. Then, exhausted and footsore but also relieved and pleased, both with the splendour of Hurricane Ridge and my night walk, I lay down to sleep. The Hot Springs could wait for the morning.

Despite my long day and late night I only slept for five hours, waking to a cloudy sky and drizzle. Over breakfast I decided that a short day would be a good idea after the rigours of yesterday. Given the weather I was to experience this was to be a sensible decision. I would probably have cut

the day short anyway. As I packed up camp I could hear the bulldozer across the creek starting up. There would soon be a road bridge across Crystal Creek, I suspected. Fine dense rain was falling as I set off through impressive Douglas firs and down the short distance to the Olympic Hot Springs, which are formed from a line of seeps beside Boulder Creek, just a small stream here. I found a series of small shallow pools dammed with crude stone walls steaming gently on the edge of the creek. I could smell sulphur and the water was warm to touch. It looked stagnant and unappealing though and I had no desire to immerse more than my fingers. At the trailhead there had been a notice warning of infectious bacteria in the water – and nude bathing! The latter, stated the rather po-faced notice, 'is not condoned by Olympic National Park'. Until the 1960s there was a resort here with cabins and piped water. I wondered what the newly restored road would bring.

Leaving the Hot Springs I wandered on through wet forest in the Boulder Creek and South Fork of Boulder Creek valleys. Much more impressive than the Hot Springs were the Lower and Upper Boulder Creek Falls; white cascades tumbling down dark mossy ravines into dark pools. I had to cross both streams. Boulder Creek was a

shin-deep paddle. The South Fork was bridged by a sturdy notched log bridge with a solid hand rail. The trail then began to climb into western hemlock forest and a series of steep, brushy meadows. This was fine country, as far as I could see through the rain and mist. The graceful hemlocks with their distinctive drooping tops were a nice contrast to the massive, solid Douglas firs with their huge column-like straight trunks. The trail led up to Appleton Pass at 5,000 feet/1524 metres where there was a campsite with cables for hanging food. It was less than four hours since I'd left the Boulder Creek Campground and I'd only walked 5.5 miles/9 kilometres. Even so, I decided to stop. The rain was lashing down, the cloud was low on the mountains and a gusty wind swept the pass. Just the weather for sleeping and resting in the tent. The guidebook said there was no water at the pass but in fact Little Oyster Lake on the edge of a meadow was only a short walk away from the campsite. This was my 70th day on the trail and I reckoned I'd walked 1052 miles/1693 kilometres though that was very much an approximation.

I spent the afternoon dozing and reading and watching the rain slash down and bounce off the ground. It was another very wet day. During the evening the wind picked up, rattling the tent.

I ventured out to check the pegs and tighten the guylines, remembering the peg that had come out at Deer Park. Looking at the map I realised that this would probably be the last high camp of the walk. The next night I hoped to be down in the rain forest and out of the mountains. I was glad I'd stopped. Dinner was an Annie's Organic Classic Macaroni and Cheese. I didn't have much choice as the only dinners I had left were varieties of Annie's organic pasta and cheese meals. Luckily I was quite fond of them.

The weather grew wilder as the night grew darker with the wind now driving the rain across the pass in great waves. Puddles were forming all around but I was on a slight slope on ground that was a little higher than the surroundings so the tent shouldn't flood. Clad in my wool and fleece clothing and lying under my quilt I was warm and cosy. I was reading *The Collector* and the descriptions of many of David Douglas's camps reminded me of how lucky I was to have modern equipment. Douglas usually travelled by horse or canoe and so could carry heavy gear. Even so it wasn't up to much of the weather he experienced and the book is full of stories of cold and wet nights, hard ground and broken sleep. After one storm, when he'd been soaked to the skin, he'd woken at midnight feeling

cold, wrapped in an inadequate blanket, so he'd lit a fire and made some tea, writing later in his journal 'If I have any zeal, for one and the first time it began to cool. Hung up my clothes to dry and lay down and slept until three o'clock'. Often he slept out with no covering but his blanket. Even when he had a tent it wasn't always much use. Of one camp, after a strong wind had blown out his fire, he wrote 'to add to my miseries, the tent was blown down about my ears, so that I lay till daylight, rolled in my wet blanket, on Pteris aquiline [fern fronds], with the drenched tent piled above me'. Food was often scarce – he lived off the land of course – or barely edible, even when he was travelling with fur traders and local Indians. He described some dried salmon – he ate a great deal of this – as tasting like 'rotten dry pine bark'. It gave him diarrhoea that incapacitated him for four days. Yet none of these experiences doused his enthusiasm for finding new plants and exploring new country. I was glad of a tent that stayed up in storms and clothing that kept out the rain but oh, how much would I have liked to explore the Pacific Northwest when it was unmapped, when there were no guidebooks, no trails, no backcountry rules and regulations, when it was possible to find unknown trees, trace the course of rivers for the first time and climb

mountains that may never have been ascended before. I think some wet nights and a soggy blanket would have been more than a fair exchange for such experiences.

Like the North Cascades, Olympic National Park seemed less organised and controlled than Glacier. The trails and campsites were more primitive and felt more natural. I knew the park was very popular but here at the end of September there were few people on the trails. The park said that nearly 40,000 people camped in the wilderness here every year. There were around 600 miles/965 kilometres of trails though so those people could spread out. Unsurprisingly given the weather I had the Appleton Pass site to myself. Also like the North Cascades I met no rangers on the trails. Here this was due to the time of year though. The ranger stations at Deer Park and Sol Duc Park were already closed for the winter.

Daylight seeped in slowly through clinging mist the next morning. The rain had stopped but the wind was shaking drips off the trees onto the tent. Today would be my last day in the high country and I would climb the last peak of the walk. I hoped I would see something but if not, well, I was used to that now. I was aiming for a spectacular sounding ridge called the High Divide. To reach it

I had first to descend 2000 feet/607 metres down to the Sol Duc River ('Sol Duc' means 'sparkling water'). A new wooden sign at the pass pointed the way and gave the distance as a precise 2.6 miles/4.2 kilometres. The rain had begun again before I set off and I wore my waterproof trousers as the trail went through dense soaking bushes that would soon have drenched my legs. In the meadows on the pass I was surprised to see lupins and harebells still in bloom. Against that many of the maples were in autumn colours, their leaves red and gold.

Down at the Sol Duc River I reached a trail junction where two young women with large packs were standing looking at a notice pinned to the trail sign that said the trail was closed between Olympic Hot Springs and the road in the Elwha valley. They asked me how long it would take to reach the Hot Springs. Their permit was for a site six miles/ten kilometres in the other direction so they decided to see if they could get to the Hot Springs and back before heading that way and I left them unpacking much of their gear so they could travel light. The climb up to the meadow filled bowl called Sol Duc Park and the High Divide was a delight as the trail wound through a mysterious misty forest of tall straight-limbed trees split by

Deer Lake

many moss-rimmed tumbling creeks that were crossed on an assortment of log bridges, some slippery and unstable, others solid and notched to give grip. One tangle of greasy logs, still held together by the rope that had once bound them into a bridge, or at least the semblance of one, was so slippery and wobbly that I backed off and forded the creek a little below them.

A notice at Sol Duc Park gave advice and instruction, pointing out that this subalpine area was fragile so care had to be taken. No wood fires were allowed and visitors were urged to stay on trails to avoid damaging the delicate plants and thin soil. Bears, it said, were common in the area so all food and garbage should be kept in sealed plastic containers. Reading this I realised that not only had I not seen any bears in the Olympics but I had seen no sign of them either. This would not change. I didn't think bears were really likely to raid camp sites here as plastic containers wouldn't be any defence against them. Special bear resistant canisters were needed for that. I guessed the instruction was a precaution intended to reduce the likelihood of bears becoming a problem. However a year after the trip bear resistant canisters became mandatory in the Sol Duc and High Divide area so maybe there had been problems with bears.

As I continued climbing past Heart Lake, whose shape gives it its name, to the High Divide there were the first hints of a clearance in the weather with brightness behind the clouds and touches of blue in the sky. The High Divide runs just above the lovely Seven Lakes Basin, which contains far more than seven timberline pools. It was a marvellous twisting ridge dotted with small mountain hemlock and subalpine fir, little rocky knolls and meadows bright with fiery autumn colours. In the guidebook Ron describes it as 'the scenic focal point of the Olympics'. To the south, across the deep Hoh River valley, rose Mount Olympus itself. I lingered on the ridge, stopping frequently for snacks and short rests, and was rewarded with a little sunshine and views of the lakes and surrounding summits. Wooded knolls, little tree groves, meadows, pools, scree slopes, rocky arêtes all came and went in swirling cloud; a mesmeric insubstantial beautiful scene. The big mountains stayed in the cloud though, hidden behind a great wall of white cloud rising out of the Hoh valley. Tantalisingly this parted slightly a few times giving brief glimpses of rocky slopes and slivers of glacier. No more of Olympus was to be revealed. Towards the western end of the ridge I reached 5474 foot/1669 metre Bogachiel Peak,

my last summit. I stared out at the misty peaks all around and thought of all the mountains I'd climbed on the PNT, named and unnamed, right back to those on the Whitefish Divide far away in Montana when the walk had been young.

From Bogachiel Peak I started my last descent from the high country, soon dropping below 5,000 feet/1524 metres for the last time. Below timberline now the trail led past little pools through the trees to Deer Lake, a scenic pool reflecting the forest and the hills with several campsites round it. A national park sign explained that the area was being restored following damage from over-use and requested campers and hikers to allow the fragile soils and vegetation to recover by sticking to trails and campsites. From Deer Lake there was a final short climb to another ridge, the Low Divide, which ranges from 3500 feet/1067 metres to 4100 feet/1250 metres. Walking along this ridge I had wonderful views of summits dark against the pink and orange sky of early evening rising above the cloud filled valleys though Olympus remained hidden. Then it was down, down, down on a wet, rocky and rooty trail that took me past the last subalpine firs, my companions for much of the walk, and the last mountain hemlocks and into big western hemlocks and Douglas firs and eventually

Rain forest in the Bogachiel River valley

the valley of the North Fork of the Bogachiel River. I was below 3,000 feet/914 metres now and would not go higher again. I was also in the rain forest. I wandered down the trail in the growing dark to the Twentyone Mile campsite where there lay the collapsed, jumbled timbers of a shelter with a patch of bare ground next to it on which I pitched the tent.

In camp I reflected on the day and the Olympic Mountains. As a final day on the heights it had been satisfying and full of light and colour. I went to sleep content. The mountains were behind me. Tomorrow, the rain forest. I was looking forward to that.

The primeval temperate rain forest in the Olympics is a strange and magical place and one of the few remaining examples of an ecosystem that once stretched from Northern California to Alaska but which has been mostly destroyed by logging. In Washington less than 10% remains. Where it is untouched the old growth rain forest is magnificent, with huge trees and lush riotous undergrowth. Moss, lichen and ferns grow everywhere. I felt that if I sat still for a few hours they would start growing on me. These are epiphytes, that is, plants that grow on other plants, and here they run rampant, covering tree trunks and dripping down from branches. For such a forest to develop two climatic factors are needed – a high annual rainfall and year round moderate temperatures. In the Olympic rain forest temperatures rarely drop below freezing in winter or rise above 80°F/27°C in summer and there is rainfall of around 12 to 14 feet/3.5-4.5 metres a year. Ironically, given the wet weather I had experienced for the last month, my day in the rain forest was one of sunshine and dryness.

The trees of the rain forest are massive and old. Sitka spruce and western hemlock are the dominant species but there are many others including some massive Douglas firs. The biggest trees may be hundreds of years old and can grow to

Trail sign in the Bogachiel River valley

250 feet/76 metres high and have circumferences of up to 60 feet/18 metres. These truly are giants. A distinctive feature of the rain forest is the nurse log phenomena. This is a decaying fallen tree or branch on which tree seedlings have taken root. As the new trees grow the nurse log rots away until they appear to be perched on stilts. The rain forest is dense and the tall trees block out much of the sky (one definition of a temperate rain forest says at least 70% of the sky must be obscured) so although the sun shone all day I was mostly in the shade. The rain forest ecosystem is so rich that it's reckoned to have a greater mass of living and dead material than anywhere else on Earth. The forest is home to much wildlife, including the largest population of Roosevelt elk. During my walk through the rain forest I saw one of these, the only elk I encountered on the whole PNT. The big deer reminded me of home, as it is a close relative of the red deer of the Scottish Highlands and looked very similar.

The rain forest in the Bogachiel River valley is some of the remotest in the Olympics as there is no road access. The much better known Hoh Rain Forest just to the south has a road partway along it plus a rain forest visitor centre and a trail that leads onto the slopes of Mount Olympus. The Bogachiel River valley is undeveloped with just a rough, often overgrown and occasionally hard to follow trail which I spent a wonderful day following with the sunshine making for a beautiful soft light in the trees. I set off amongst big Douglas firs but soon reached the first gigantic Sitka spruce and some western red cedar that were almost as big. By comparison the western hemlocks, which would have seemed massive anywhere else, seemed quite normal in girth though just as tall. Looking at the magnificent Sitka spruce, some of the most amazing trees I had ever seen, I thought of David Douglas back in the 1830s collecting its seed and introducing the tree to Britain, where it is now best known as a tree of gloomy plantations, packed together in rows and with no undergrowth. The contrast between those sad farmed trees and these spectacular and glorious giants growing in such a rich forest was enormous. This was how a forest should be. The plantations of home were not even a pale imitation.

Below the giants the wet undergrowth shone in the sunlight that filtered down through the high, far-off forest canopy. There were maples here and rowans, clad in autumn reds and yellows so the forest was awash with colour. The trail was often muddy and rough with roots and there were many creeks to splash through. At trail junctions there

Sitka spruce in the Bogacheil River rain forest

were wooden trail signs, covered with moss and rotting back into the forest, as were the occasional boardwalks across some of the muddiest sections.

At times the trail touched the edge of the North Fork and later the Bogachiel River, suddenly emerging into sunshine and brightness and views up the rivers to the mountains. Mostly though I was in the slightly unreal world of the rain forest. I passed other campsites, some with lean-to shelters, but saw no other people and no sign that anyone had been this way for a while. How fast I wondered did footprints disappear and vegetation grow back over the trail. Quite quickly, I expected.

The trail led out of the National Park and into unprotected forest. The first signs of logging came before the park boundary, where there were mossy stumps from a time before the park came into being. Soon I reached a trailhead. On the Forest Service notice board I found a note from Kris telling me which site she was on at the Bogachiel State Park campround, where we had agreed to meet. Further down the road I had reception on my phone and rang her to say I should be there in about an hour. That was the one and only time I made a phone call while hiking. I arrived at the campground well after dark and was delighted when Kris produced hot chilli beans with bread and cheese, a delicious meal. The campground was set amidst big Sitka spruce but the natural feeling was somewhat destroyed by the sound of traffic on a nearby highway.

I had another route decision to make here, the last one of the walk. I'd made up my mind which I would choose many days before however. To reach the coast I could either follow the route described in the guidebook, which ran through logged forest on roads and trails for some 23 miles/36 kilometres and then followed the coast for 39 miles/63 kilometres, or walk on paved roads to the coast, a distance of 20 miles/32 kilometres, and then along the coast for another 25 miles/40 kilometres. Ron's guidebook description of the 'maze of clear-cuts and logging roads' in the forest was unappealing. I'd had enough of such country. The road would be faster with no route-finding difficulties and would take me through the town of Forks. I knew I would rather visit a town than see more destroyed and damaged forest. Missing some of the coast didn't bother me, not now, not so close to the finish. My mind was beginning to leap ahead beyond the walk to a different life that I hadn't thought about it since I'd set off. I felt restless and disturbed. I wanted to finish and yet I didn't because I knew I would feel sad as well as satisfied when the adventure was over. There was no going back though, no way of returning to having the walk stretch out in front of me and not having to think of what happened afterwards. 'Afterwards' was almost here. I would go via Forks. I noted that Li's maps showed a 'possible future route' that would run through the forest to Forks and then follow roads to the coast so it maybe that the PNT will officially run through the town one day.

Kris left to drive into Forks, where we would meet for lunch. I hiked down the highway into the little town. I knew that it was the setting for the extremely popular Twilight books and films, none of which I had read or seen, but I hadn't realised just how much the stories had taken over the town. Everything was Twilight themed, often quite imaginatively. I especially liked a roadside stall selling Twilight firewood – logs that keep evil vampires away – and a restaurant offering Twilight pizza. I met Kris and we had lunch in the Twilight restaurant where copies of the Twilight themed menu could be purchased for $4. Kris bought one for her daughter Leanne, who was keen on the books. I remembered she had been reading one on the journey to Montana, so, so long ago. Twilight has clearly been a boon for a little town that once depended on logging, an industry in decline. From Forks I followed more paved roads to Mora Campground on the edge of the coastal strip of the Olympic National Park. The day was sunny and

The Pacific Ocean at Rialto Beach, Olympic National Park

Celebrating reaching the Pacific, Olympic National Park

clear again and I could look back over the logged forest to the now distant Olympic Mountains shining in the sun. One I thought was probably Mount Olympus itself. Kris was already set up in the campground, which lay amongst more massive Sitka spruce and western red cedar and, unlike Bogachiel State Park, was quiet.

I knew that the coastal section of the PNT went round some headlands that were only passable at low tide so I'd asked Kris to get me a tide table. She'd done so and had talked to a ranger about walking the coast. Low tide the next day was 12.52 a.m. To be at Cape Johnson, the first obstacle, to take advantage of it I would need to start hiking

at 7 a.m. Being early would not be a problem – I could wait – but being late would be so I decided I'd better get up at 5 a.m., the earliest on the whole walk. I'm not an early riser and much prefer walking long into the night to starting out early. I had often read that good or serious walkers do most of their daily mileage before midday and had accepted that in that case I was happy to be a bad, unserious one. This time I really did have to start early though, not to be good or serious but to be safe.

Kris had also brought a bear resistant container, which I needed to protect my food against racoons and to comply with park regulations. So determined is the national park on this that canisters can be borrowed for free from ranger stations. The park regulations said 'Along the coast, especially at Cape Alava and Sand Point in the Ozette area, years of heavy use, feeding of wildlife, and improper food storage have habituated raccoons to stealing human food. Raccoons are clever, resourceful and aggressive. They can climb ropes, hang from tree branches and leap long distances. Raccoons have learned how to work toggles and zippers, and can unscrew containers.' The only permitted alternative to a canister was a hard container such as a 5-gallon paint bucket with snap fastened lid and this had

to be hung from a high branch. A bear canister seemed an easier option. These are quite heavy – around 3 pounds/1.4 kilograms – and awkward to pack. However, although I would only have one camp along the coast, I didn't want to lose my food to racoons or be fined by a ranger so I'd decided I would carry a canister. In the past I'd carried one for five weeks on a 500 mile/800 kilometre walk in the High Sierra in California so I should be able to manage one for 2 days.

During the night the weather changed and I woke to an overcast sky and a gusty wind. I walked a last two road miles to Rialto Beach at the mouth of the Quillayute River and there was the Pacific Ocean, wild and white and windswept and strewn with sea stacks and islets; a powerful presence that belied its name. I felt a sudden surge of excitement. I had hiked from the Rockies to the Pacific. In a sense this was the end of the walk even though I would walk up the coast that day and the next. Here on the shores of the Pacific I had come to the edge of the USA. I paddled into the surf and felt the ocean tugging at my legs. Out on a sandbank lay a harbour seal. Gulls wheeled overhead.

Kris walked a little way up the coast with me then returned to her car to drive round to the nearest car park to the end of the PNT. She would walk down the coast to meet me the next day. The coast lived up to its name of the Wilderness Coast, being magnificently wild and scenic. The rock scenery was stunning with masses of sea stacks of every shape and size, many with trees growing on them, out in the ocean and on the shore plus big rock walls protruding out from the cliffs, often with arches cut through them. The sky remained cloudy and the wind strong, whirling sea spray into the air and making distant views hazy.

The walking was mixed, ranging from firm sandy beaches to greasy pebbles and boulders and rippled, wave smoothed rock terraces that were as difficult to cross as anything in the mountains and

My cousin Kris on the Pacific coast, Olympic National Park

where I was very glad of my trekking poles. I'd have fallen a few times without them. There were many huge logs too, both ones that had washed up and ones that had fallen from the forest above as the ocean slowly eroded the coast. I had to negotiate tangles of these, which was slow and awkward and needed care as I was often stepping from log to log several feet above the ground. A few times I had to remove my pack in order to squeeze through narrow gaps between large boulders and logs wedged against them.

As well as my trekking poles I was glad of my binoculars as there were many birds. I probably used them more on the last two days than on all the rest of the walk. Out on the ocean a big flock of brown pelicans flew past, low over the water. I had never seen wild pelicans before. They looked ungainly but were flying strongly into the wind. Also on the ocean were delicate looking, pretty little harlequin ducks, black tough-looking cormorants and a raft of equally dark surf scoters. The forest came right down to the edge of the bluffs and cliffs above the shore and looking inland I watched a bald eagle flying low above the trees. A heron fished in a tidal pool. This meeting of forest and ocean was rich country. Unsurprisingly much of it is protected in the Quillayute Needles National Wildlife Refuge as

well as the national park.

I reached the cliffs of Cape Johnson half an hour before low tide, perfect timing. Walking below the cliffs took time as much of it was on wet, slippery seaweed covered boulders. There were many rock pools and the surf was pounding the rocks not far away. I would not have liked to do this section with time pressing. It was very obvious that it was usually under water. Once round the headland I was surprised to see three black-tailed deer out on the rocks. They wandered past me unafraid whilst I took their photographs.

Sandy beaches and easier walking then led to Cedar Creek where I camped in the edge of the forest with a view out across the ocean. It was a fine site and the last camp of the walk. I was glad it was in such a wild and beautiful spot. Making camp felt like a ritual. I had done it many times, often barely thinking about it, but this last one was special. I would never again do this on the PNT. I cooked over wood in my little stove, thinking what a success it had been. Then I thought of the much greater success of the whole walk. Tomorrow I would reach the end. I found it hard to believe. Part of me still thought that this is what I did, that I walked each day through nature and camped each night. I could barely imagine doing anything

different. I remembered this was the effect a really long walk, one lasting at least a couple of weeks, had on me. Although I had done many superb trips in recent years, including hiking the amazing GR20 path on the island of Corsica in the Mediterranean Sea, trekking in the Himalayas and ski touring and building igloos in Yellowstone National Park and the Wind River Range it had been ten years since I had last hiked such a long distance trail. I had missed it and felt as though I had rediscovered an important part of my life.

That evening I sat on the edge of the forest and watched the ocean and the birds. A huge raft of scoters, a hundred plus I estimated, bobbed on the water, a dark patch riding the waves. On the beach a sandpiper prodded the sand and glaucous-winged gulls stood staring. The ocean pounded the shore and I could hear the roar and crash of the surf yet at the same time I felt relaxed and the place felt peaceful.

I was asleep early and although excited at the thought of reaching the finish I slept for over eleven hours. I didn't need an early start as low tide was 2.14 p.m. and I had more headlands to go round. The wind had dropped and the clouds had thinned, revealing a hazy moon high overhead. I had just 15 miles/24 kilometres left to walk.

Sea stacks in the Pacific Ocean, Olympic National Park

Not far from Cedar Creek I came on a headland where an old broken down rope ladder with dangling broken wooden rungs hung down a steep muddy slope. This was a remnant of a World War II Coast Guard trail and the only way to safely cross this headland. I hauled myself up the slippery slope using the old rope ladder for holds then plunged on through easier overgrown terrain to the crest of the 200 foot/61 metre headland. The climb required quite an effort. The Pacific Northwest Trail was not winding down easily. Once back down steeply to sea level the walking eased for a while on a sandy beach but then grew much more difficult on a long stretch of greasy, kelp-covered, rounded smooth rocks, wonderfully described by Ron in the guidebook as 'slippery cannonball-sized ankle-sprainers'. These led to Yellow Banks, a long stretch of lovely smooth sand at the far end of which lay the headland I needed to round at low tide. I arrived an hour too early. A quick venture along the rocks without my pack showed that it was impassable. I spent the time bird watching. The clouds had cleared and the sun was shining so the clarity was far better than the previous day. Two more bald eagles flew overhead and as well as all the birds I'd seen the day before there were black oystercatchers, western gulls, Canada geese and ravens on the shore. Scanning the ocean I spotted a seal bobbing in the water.

Finally low tide arrived and I cautiously scrambled over the wet rocks below the ragged, half-collapsed cliffs, all too aware of the ocean pounding away close by. The way through the big boulders right at the tip of the headland was via a dark tunnel in the rocks with trees growing on its roof. Once this obstacle was safely negotiated I could relax. A few hikers heading in the other direction passed me then I spotted Kris coming towards me. Soon afterwards we reached Cape Alava. There really was no land further west. My Pacific Northwest Trail hike was over. I felt elated, relieved and sad at the same time. This really was the end. Kris produced a small bottle of champagne and I toasted the walk, toasted the wilderness, the trees, the mountains, the animals and birds, the trails and campsites, even the rain and wind. A wonderful summer had come to an end. All that was left was to turn away from the magical coast and walk through the forest to the road and Kris's car. This time I would accept a lift. There was no more walking to be done.

Journey's End. Cape Alava, the western terminus of the Pacific Northwest Trail

AFTERMATH

Celebrating at the end of the trail

The impact of a long walk takes time to settle in to the mind. For months after the walk events and ideas would suddenly come to me and I would think back to those days on the trail and reconsider them. Reading my journals whilst writing this book I was surprised at some of the feelings expressed. I couldn't remember feeling like that. From a distance my view of aspects of the walk had changed. What seemed important at the time sometimes seemed inconsequential in retrospect. When I think of the PNT my mind fills with images of giant trees (for some reason those glorious trees always come first); wild mountains; lovely campsites; peaceful lakes; rushing torrents; bald eagles soaring overhead; bear scat on the trail; the spine-chilling call of a loon; a narrow trail winding across a mountain slope above a mist-filled valley; everything, in fact, that makes up the beautiful wilderness of the Pacific Northwest. Forgotten are the highway walks; the trudges through logged forests; the rain; the sore feet; the mosquitoes because, when it comes down

to it, these are unimportant. The meaning of the walk is in the days and weeks spent in wild places; in the feeling of rightness and oneness with nature that comes with time spent in the outdoors; the feeling of fitness, both physical and mental, that comes when every day is spent walking and active; and in the feeling of restoration and completeness that came with immersing myself in one simple but profound activity – walking in the wilderness – for a whole summer.

The Pacific Northwest Trail walk is now part of me, an experience that is deep within me and which I will recall often. I am grateful to have had the opportunity to spend a summer hiking this marvellous route.

Where now for the PNT though? Official recognition as a National Scenic Trail means money and expertise for trail building and development. An official trail corridor will be set by the United States Forest Service. Inevitably there will be compromises and route choices that don't please everyone. I hope, though, that the new route will stay true to the dreams and vision of Ron Strickland when he conceived of the trail all those years ago. I think it is appropriate for Ron to have the last word:

Beginning in 1970, my vision for the PNT has

A peaceful camp

always been that it will provide hikers with a superbly-uncompromising walking experience. Over the decades in which I planned the PNT's route, hikers and volunteers always asked me to "stay high for the views." As time goes on, that philosophy will increasingly be subverted by regulatory, commercial, and financial pressures. Yet we must always think about the Pacific Northwest Trail in light of the long term goal of creating the best of the best. I would like all of our hikers, volunteers, administrators, and land owners to ask themselves, 'What can I do to ensure that the PNT is truly ready for its fiftieth anniversary in 2020?'

APPENDICES

Statistics: Distance, Camping, Weather

By keeping a running total of my daily distance I ended up with a total of 1141.71 miles/1837.4 kilometres, which is ridiculously precise. This was compiled from the distances given in the guidebook and on Li's maps and by counting the distance on various maps. I didn't always follow either Ron's or Li's route exactly and sometimes I was on neither. I reckon my total is probably only accurate to 10% either way at best – a longer distance is more likely than a shorter one. Without recording the route on a GPS it's almost impossible to get a remotely accurate distance for cross country sections.

The walk took 75 days, of which 7 were rest days. On the 68 days on which I walked I averaged around 16.8 miles/27 kilometres per day, which is remarkably consistent with my daily averages on other long walks. That distance per day seems to suit me. The longest day was 32 miles/52 kilometres between Deer Park and Olympic Hot Springs in Olympic National Park, the shortest was the next day when I walked just 5.5 miles/9 kilometres from the Hot Springs to Appleton Pass. I never hiked more than 30 miles/48 kilometres on any other day. I did hike between 20 and 30 miles/32 and 48 kilometres on 13 days. In time I was usually out between 8-10 hours a day. The 32 mile/52 kilometre day took 16.5 hours. Only on 4 other days was I out for more than 12 hours.

I spent 60 nights camping and 15 in accommodation. My highest camp was on Bald Mountain in the Pasayten Wilderness at 7300 feet/2225 metres. The lowest camp was the last one at Cedar Creek on the Pacific coast, which was barely above sea level.

The weather was very mixed, which was expected on a walk that took me from the interior of the continent to the ocean, and I had to deal with thunderstorms, heatwaves and many days of low cloud and rain. The walk began mostly dry and finished mostly wet. In the first 49 days there was only significant rain on 6 days, and a little drizzle on a few others. In the last 26 days there was rain on 19 days, often heavy. In those first 49 days the humidity level was usually quite low, with any rain quickly followed by dry, sunny conditions. Every morning I recorded the relative humidity and it only reached 100% eight times in that first period and sometimes dropped as low as 50%. In the last 26 days it was 100% every day bar one – when it was 99.4%. Often I camped and hiked in wet mist even when it wasn't raining. I learnt later that the weather that September in Washington State, where I spent the whole month, was the wettest for thirty years.

Unlike when backpacking at home in the Scottish Highlands I usually camped in forests so wind wasn't a problem. In fact I only had three really windy camps during the whole trip. Whilst this meant the tent didn't often have to stand up to big winds and I wasn't kept awake by thrashing nylon it also meant that there was nothing to remove condensation on humid nights so the tent

was often damp in the morning.

Temperatures were overall warmer than I expected, especially in September when many frosty nights are usual in the mountains. In fact the temperature only fell below zero twice the whole trip and then only slightly with the lowest temperature being -1.1°C/30°F. During the first part of the walk daytime temperatures were often in the 30s°C/80s°F and staying cool and hydrated was the main problem. For the last month the temperatures were twenty degrees and more lower and the rain and high humidity meant it felt chilly much of the time.

Navigation

Navigation was often quite difficult, for many different reasons. Many times I had to find the line of an old trail, select the best route through dense forest or choose the right one in a maze of forest roads. My Silva 7NL compass was an essential tool and was used often. Of course good maps were required too and I had topographic maps in two forms. Li Brannfors had hiked the PNT in 2009 and recorded his route on his GPS unit (which meant carrying loads of batteries – I'm glad someone else did this!) and sent me A4 print-outs of topographic maps with his route and alternatives marked,

The smartphone/GPS

with distances between points. These maps were my main ones and were carried, folded, in an Aloksak bag in a shirt pocket for quick access. I also had ViewRanger software with topo maps on my HTC Desire phone, which had a GPS function. ViewRanger worked well and provided all the features of a stand-alone GPS. I used it whenever I found locating the correct route with map and

compass difficult as it made route-finding much easier and quicker. A few times I used it to find junctions with disused trails hidden in dense vegetation. To find these junctions I would switch on ViewRanger and follow the route on the map until I had reached the right point. Usually there was no sign of the trail but after I had followed its line with the GPS for a short distance signs of it

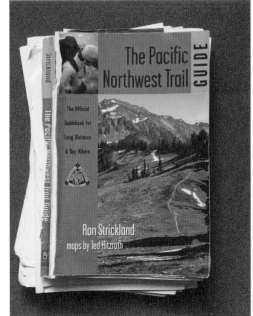

The guidebook after the walk

would appear.

I also had Ron Strickland's PNT guidebook, which I sliced into sections so I didn't have to carry the whole volume. I often read the route descriptions over breakfast to have an overview of the day and for Ron's entertaining comments. Occasionally I referred to the description during the day if I was puzzled by the relationship between the map and the terrain. I didn't bother with the guidebook maps as these are in black and white and Li's were full colour.

I also carried larger scale national park and Forest Service maps so I had an overview of areas and could place myself in the landscape and identify surrounding features. The Forest Service maps were sometimes useful when following logging roads as well.

Food

Some long distance hikers like to plan their food supplies down to every calorie and carefully balance carbohydrates, protein and fat (though which should predominate can lead to huge debates). I don't do that. I know from experience that around 2 lbs/1kg of food a day will be enough as long as I don't carry low calorie items. I also like buying food along the way, which can be interesting and also supports local communities. This did mean that sometimes I had to buy more than I needed, in which case I simply mailed the surplus ahead in my running supply box.

For breakfast I usually ate muesli or granola with dried milk powder, and sugar if it wasn't sweetened, mixing it with cold water. 4-5oz/112-140 grams per day was plenty. A few times when I couldn't get enough muesli or granola I bought instant oatmeal, to which I added dried fruit. During the day I ate trail mix, which I made up from a variety of items – mostly dried fruit, nuts and seeds with occasionally chocolate chips, butterscotch chips or M&Ms; grain and dried fruit

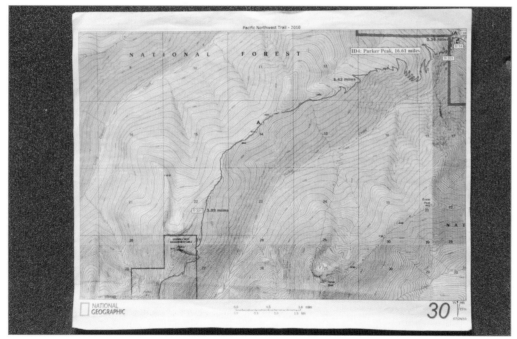

One of Li's maps

bars and sometimes chocolate (though not in hot weather when it makes a sticky mess). For variety I occasionally carried tortillas, thought I usually ended up eating these with dinner. Rather than having one long lunch stop I snacked frequently throughout the day, often while hiking.

Evening meals were dehydrated all-in-one dinners, usually pasta based, as I find this fills me up and seems to provide energy the next day. The main alternative to pasta was instant potato, which was good on very long days as it didn't require any cooking or simmering and so could provide a meal very quickly. Some of the specialist backpacking meals just required adding hot water, but then waiting 10-15 minutes for them to hydrate. Meals bought from supermarkets and grocery stores usually needed simmering for 5-10 minutes. Anything that took longer than 10 minutes to cook I left on the store shelf. To bulk out the meals I often added cheese. Except in the hottest weather when it often started to liquefy I found that hard Cheddar kept well in the pack. I also carried tiny quantities of herbs and spices to pep up bland meals. Most of the time I had packet soups too – instant cup-a-soups or 5 minute simmer ones – which were good to eat soon after making camp as they were warming and restored liquid and salt. I didn't bother with desserts. If still peckish after my main meal I'd raid my day snacks.

For drinks I had instant coffee and hot chocolate, which I often mixed together as the coffee was often not that nice on its own, plus spiced apple cider. Mostly though I just drank water. Not once did I stop during the day and make a hot drink, not even when the weather was wet and chilly.

Equipment

I chose my equipment with care as it needed to handle a wide variety of weather conditions while being light and compact. On a long distance walk gear takes quite a battering so it needs to be tough. I'm not an ultralight minimalist hiker so I didn't go for the very lightest items but I did want to keep the weight low. I wanted enough clothing to be able to stay warm and comfortable sitting round in camp and gear that should easily last the whole walk without needing special care or pampering. Overall I like equipment I can mostly forget about because it does its job.

Footwear

Footwear is the key to comfortable walking. I like lightweight flexible footwear, even in rough terrain, and prefer shoes to boots so for most of the walk I wore Inov8 Terroc shoes, which I found comfortable with good grip and which weighed just 25oz/698 grams a pair. I went through two pairs, neither of which was completely worn out. During the last month of the walk the shoes were soaked for days on end but still felt fine. Only in the very hottest weather did I find them uncomfortable. Then my feet swelled enough with the heat that even without socks the shoes were too tight. The answer, I knew, was a pair of sandals but, to save weight, I foolishly hadn't brought a pair so I was very pleased to find some Merrell ones in the little town of Eureka nine days into the walk. I wore them on the hottest days and in towns, around camp and on some of the road walks. The extra weight of 24oz/688 grams was well worthwhile for the freedom they gave my feet in the heat.

In the Terrocs I wore merino wool Teko Light Hiking Socks. Two pairs just lasted the whole trip, though both had holes in them by the end. In dry weather I could rinse out the socks and dry them on the pack. In the wet weather I wore the same wet pair for a week and more at a time, keeping the dry ones for tent wear. Even when wet the socks were comfortable and warm.

Pack & Storage

I began the trek with a GoLite Pinnacle (33oz/935grams), a pack I'd used successfully on several TGO Challenge walks across the Scottish Highlands. And for three weeks it was comfortable and stable and I was happy with it. But then the shoulder straps began to twist and deform and became quite uncomfortable. At the same time holes appeared in the fabric and straps and seams started to tear. Concerned that the pack wouldn't last the rest of the trip and not wanting to carry what was now quite an uncomfortable pack I contacted GoLite who immediately offered to replace it. I still had to nurse it through another ten days until I reached a Post Office and could collect the new pack, a GoLite Quest. Although the capacity was the same at 72 litres the Quest was some 16oz/465 grams heavier than the Pinnacle at 49oz/1400 grams. I didn't notice the extra weight though. I was just happy to have a comfortable pack. The Quest was in fine condition at the end of the walk and I was very pleased with it. As both packs had just about the same usage in time and conditions, though the Quest had to cope with much more wet weather, I can only think that the Pinnacle was a rogue pack that slipped through quality control.

Both packs had excellent pockets for organising gear. The big rear pockets were good for clothing, especially wet waterproofs. The mesh side pockets held water and fuel bottles and the hipbelt pockets mini binoculars and snacks. The Quest also had a lid pocket, in which I kept small items like GPS/phone, headlamp, lunch food, notebook and knife.

For packing water sensitive gear I used Pod Ultralite Drysacs and Lifeventure Dri-Store bags (3 in total weighing 4.7oz/133 grams). Both types were made from waterproof nylon with taped seams and roll tops. I used various sizes for my sleeping bag, spare clothing and other items. By squeezing the air out I could reduce the size of packed items more than with a conventional stuffsack. I didn't use a pack liner and my sleeping bag in the 15 litre Lifeventure Dri-Store was packed at the bottom of the pack every day. In wet weather the outside of the stuffsack was often wet at the end of the day but the sleeping bag was always dry inside.

I also had three clear Aloksak waterproof bags in different sizes, which I used for maps, notebook and phone. These super tough plastic bags are very flexible so I could easily fold the large one with the map for storage in a shirt pocket. They also weighed little; the total for all three being 1.6oz/46grams.

Tent

Wanting a shelter that could be pitched with my trekking poles I took a GoLite Shangri-La 1, a simple tapered ridge tent, plus the Shangri-La 1 Nest mesh inner tent, with a combined weight of 34oz/963 grams. The tent could be pitched with just six pegs but I added four more for the extra guylines I attached. One of these, at the front peak, was very useful as pegging it out tightened the ridgeline for a tauter pitch and also meant I could open the whole front of the tent without it collapsing. The side guys were useful for stability on the rare windy nights and for giving better separation with the mesh inner but I didn't often use them. The rear guyline wasn't really needed. Four more pegs were needed to pitch the Nest.

I brought the Nest to keep off the mosquitoes I knew could be a problem early on in the walk and it did this well. Indeed, on some clear warm nights I used the Nest on its own, which gave me a good view of the stars and the landscape whilst keeping off the bugs. Once the mosquitoes faded away, from mid-August onwards, I had intended using the Nest as a groundsheet only. In fact I only did this on a few nights as I found that in wet weather the high waterproof walls of the Nest kept splashes of rain coming under the edge of the tent

and condensation running down the tent walls off my gear as well as stopping gear sliding off the groundsheet onto muddy ground.

Overall the Shangri-La 1 combination performed well and I grew to like it very much. It was just the right size for myself and all my gear and in heavy rain there was space to use the stove in the vestibule. It stood up to the few windy nights well and was in good condition at the end of the walk.

Sleeping Quilt

As the freezing temperatures I expected in September never materialised I ended up taking a quilt that was much warmer than I needed. This was a GoLite Ultralite 3-Season, rated to -7°C/19.4°F and weighing 25oz/708 grams. I would have been better off with the 20.5oz/580 gram 1+ Season Quilt, rated to +4°C/39°F and wearing clothes in it on the coldest nights. Only ever having used a quilt on a couple of nights before the trip taking one was a bit of an experiment. The Ultralite quilt had straps underneath for attaching it to a mat so there are no cold spots at the sides and I found these useful on the few nights where the temperature fell below +5°C/41°F. However I never needed to sleep in clothes and usually just draped the quilt

over me. Overall the quilt was very comfortable.

Insulating Mat

Suspecting I would often be sleeping on hard-packed bare ground I wanted an insulating mat that provided good cushioning. Inflatable air beds are best for this so I took a Pacific Outdoor Equipment Ether Elite 6 2/3 (11oz/312 grams). It proved supremely comfortable yet weighed less than most thinner mats and packed up very small as it only had thin strips of insulation inside. In the mostly above freezing temperatures it was warm enough. My joy in this air bed only lasted 47 days however as on the 47th night it sprang a leak, just as the stormy weather of September began. A tiny pinhole along a seam was the cause. I covered it with glue from the tiny repair kit supplied with the mat and it was okay for a few nights but then started to deflate again, though only slowly. I added more glue and then a patch but the leak continued, spreading, I suspect, along the seam. After many days of blowing up the mat every 3 or 4 hours each night I gave up and borrowed an old Therm-A-Rest Ultralite ¾ self-inflating mat, which I used for the last 10 days. This didn't feel as comfortable as the Ether 6 when lying in the tent but I slept on it just as well. It weighed rather more at 17oz/480 grams

and was slightly bulkier when packed.

At the last minute I also took a thin piece of closed cell foam, the OMM Duo Mat, to use as a sit mat and under my feet on cold, wet ground in the tent. At 5oz/143 grams it added little to my load and having a dry seat was very welcome during wet weather.

Stove, Kitchen & Water

The Caldera Ti-Tri Inferno stove was one of the great successes of the walk as I really enjoyed using it. I took it because it can be used with wood and I knew I would be camping in forests much of the time. It also comes with a tiny ultralight alcohol burner for those times when wood was wet or unavailable. For the first six weeks of the walk I used wood regularly as there were always tiny dry twigs and wood chips around my camp sites. Having a mini camp fire was fun and also efficient. Water boiled more quickly with wood than alcohol and I could also control the heat for simmering, something impossible with alcohol. In wet weather I did use alcohol, which I was able to buy in every town along the way, as HEET de-icer or rubbing alcohol. The titanium Caldera Cone and inner cone for use with wood were both in good condition at the end of the walk. The drinks can alcohol burner

My favourite gear – the wood burning stove

was a little dented but still usable. The whole unit weighed 8oz/225 grams. I carried a Light My Fire Firesteel (0.9oz/26 grams) for lighting the stove. It has the advantage of not being affected by the damp. As a back-up I carried a small butane lighter weighing about the same.

I used my nineteen year old Evernew 0.9 litre Titanium Pan (4.9oz/132 grams with lid) with the Ti-Tri Inferno and it was as good as ever. My mug was an MSR 0.6 litre titanium pot (2.9oz/82 grams). One advantage of using the Inferno with wood is that I could boil water in both pots as they sit on tent pegs inserted in the windshield high above the fire. With alcohol only the Evernew pan could be used as the pan has to fit precisely into the cone. I also had two spoons (in case I lost one) weighing 0.9oz/26grams together. One was titanium and had a long handle for eating out of deep food packets. The other was aluminium and normal length. I've broken too many plastic spoons to take one on a long walk.

For water I set off with two rollup Platypus 2 litre bottles (total weight 2.6oz/74 grams) for camp use and a GoLite 700ml wide-mouthed bottle (2.8oz/79 grams) for on the trail. Being wide-mouthed the GoLite bottle was also useful when taking water from shallow trickles and seeps. It proved far too small in the hot weather of the first six weeks however as water sources were often many miles apart so I supplemented it with a 1 litre soft drinks bottle that weighed about the same. For much of the walk I drank the water straight from streams and springs without treatment. However in the Kettle River Range and the Okanogan lowlands there were many cattle and water sources were often filthy. To treat this water I used a SteriPen Adventurer Opti (3.6oz/103 grams), which uses UV light. It was easy and quick to use, far simpler than any filter. I presume it worked as I didn't get sick and some of the water was badly polluted.

Clothing

With weather ranging from very hot days to stormy days with sleet and near freezing temperatures my clothing had to be very versatile. It also needed to be tough and fast drying. Apart from my cotton sun hat it was mostly made from synthetic fabrics plus a couple of woollen items.

The one garment I wore every day of the walk was a polyester Paramo Katmai Light Shirt (7.3oz/207 grams). This proved tough and comfortable. It survived all the bushwhacking and stayed remarkably clean and uncreased even after ten days without washing. It also wicked quite well and dried very fast when damp. In the heat the wide sleeves could easily be rolled up. I kept my folded map, compass and other items in the spacious pockets. Overall this was the best hiking shirt I had used. Under other garments it was fine except in the coolest, wettest weather when it became clammy and felt damp and cold against the skin. After experiencing this a few times I wore a merino wool Icebreaker Ultralite 140 T Shirt (5.7oz/162 grams) under it, which made for a comfortable combination. Mostly, though, the t-shirt was worn in the tent, if at all.

In the hot weather and open country I wore an old pair of GoLite Skyrunner shorts (4.7oz/132 grams) on my legs. These were comfortable and lasted the whole walk, though the inner brief did eventually fall apart. For bushwhacking and in cooler weather I wore Montane Terra Lite trousers (11oz/311 grams) over the shorts and these were excellent, surviving the lashing vegetation and keeping out wind and light rain. As spares and for camp use I carried a pair of The North Face Seamless Briefs, made from polypropylene and weighing a mere 1.8oz/50g.

In breezy but dry weather I wore a GoLite Kings Canyon windshirt (4.9oz/139 grams) over the Paramo shirt. This zip-fronted hooded windshirt worked fine and I wore it often. The hood was useful when my head felt a little chilly.

For rain I had a Rab Demand Pull-On eVent waterproof top (10oz/283 grams) and GoLite Reed overtrousers (3.9oz/110grams). The Rab smock was superb, keeping me dry during the days of rain and breathing well. I was never more than slightly damp underneath it. The hood gave good protection and the chest pocket was big enough for a map. For lightweight backpacking in wet places I think this is one of the best waterproofs around. The overtrousers were worn less often but worked fine when they were needed, which was more for pushing through wet vegetation than to keep off rain. As the rain often came straight down my legs didn't get very damp even without the overtrousers.

For warmwear I took an old Jack Wolfskin Gecko microfleece sweater (7.9oz/225 grams) and a Mont-Bell Ultra Light Inner Down Jacket (7.5oz/212 grams). The Gecko was worn most evenings and mornings and while walking during the coolest weather. It was well-worn at the start of the walk but still looked fine by the end. Most of the time the Gecko was the only warm garment I needed, making the down jacket rather a luxury. I used the latter as a pillow every night but only wore it in the coldest weather. Given the wet weather a synthetic filled garment would have been a better choice, though it would have weighed more. I never got the down jacket wet though and I was never cold.

For the sun I took a cotton T3 Tilley Hat (5.5oz/156 grams), which I also found effective against rain showers and for keeping vegetation off my face and out of my hair when bushwhacking. For cool weather I had a merino wool Smartwool Cuffed Beanie (1.9oz/53 grams), which was warm and comfortable while packing away into a tiny bundle and weighing little. I also carried a pair of old polypro liner gloves (1.4oz/40 grams) that I never wore, though I almost did a couple of times.

Accessories

My carbon fibre Pacer Poles (18.6oz/528 grams) were used every day of the trip as trekking poles and every night I camped as tent poles and were excellent in both cases. They were particularly useful when bushwhacking for holding vegetation out of the way and stopping me falling when I stumbled over a hidden rock or root.

Later in the walk as daylight hours shrank I often made camp in the dark. Sometimes I walked in the dark for several hours too (on my longest day I walked in the dark for seven hours and made camp at 2 a.m.!) For light I took a Petzl Tikka XP headlamp (2.7oz/76 grams), which worked perfectly throughout the walk.

I don't actually find much use for a knife blade when backpacking and use scissors far more often. The tiny Leatherman Style CS multi-tool (1.5oz/42 grams) has a pair of the best scissors I've found on a lightweight knife plus a sharp blade and a few other tools. It worked fine throughout the walk. Thinking I might need a larger blade for cutting kindling and sticks for the fire, at the last minute I added a Tool Logic SLR knife (2.7oz/78 grams), which has a lock blade plus a Fire Steel, so I had a spare, and a whistle in the handle. I did use the blade for kindling but more often for

opening food packets. The Style CS would have been adequate on its own.

For recording weather conditions such as wind speed, overnight temperature and humidity I carried the Kestrel 4500 Weather Station (3.8oz/109 grams), which is easy to use and very efficient. I ran it on old headlamp batteries and was surprised when batteries that barely produced a flicker of light were rated as having over 80% power by the Kestrel. They lasted for weeks too.

On the trail the HTC Desire smartphone (5.6oz/160 grams) was mainly used as a GPS though I sometimes used it as an e-reader in camp and on boring road sections. In towns I used it to send emails and reports and photos to TGO, update my blog, and even, occasionally, as a phone. I rarely got a hint of a phone signal in the wilds and never an internet connection. Overall I found the Desire useful and a versatile replacement for a standalone GPS. The phone battery lasted about eight hours and I carried two spare batteries plus a Freeloader Pico solar charger (1.7oz/49 grams), which lived on top of my pack. I found the Pico would half-charge the phone after two to three days of sunny weather. Of course I was often in the shade of the forest and it was often cloudy. I would expect it to be more efficient in hotter more open places.

For a journal I used a small notebook with sewn-in pages and a water-resistant cover plus a couple of pens with waterproof ink and a pencil (total weight 6.9oz/195 grams). I kept notes on everything and filled one and a half notebooks.

Other small items included two cotton bandannas (1.9oz/54 grams), which served as general purpose cloths, Silva 7NL compass (0.8oz/24 grams), TechTrail Alterra altimeter watch (2.6oz/74 grams), dark glasses (2.5oz/70 grams), first aid kit (5.3oz/150 grams), gear repair kit (3oz/85 grams), wash/tooth kit (toothbrush, toothpaste, hand sanitizer) (3.5oz/100 grams) and mini binoculars (5.3oz/149 grams).

Weight

The total weight of all my gear including cameras was approximately 27lbs/12.2kg. I usually wore or carried separately around 6.4lbs/2.9kg so my pack's base weight – without food, fuel or water – was about 20.5lbs/9.3kg. To this must be added consumables – mainly food and fuel and occasionally water plus maps, guidebook pages and paperback books – which weighed around 2.5lbs/1.1kg a day. With a full ten days supplies my pack weighed around 45lbs/20.5kg. The most it weighed was around 55lbs/25kg when I was also

carrying 5 quarts/litres of water, which was rare.

Photography

Photography on a long walk is always a compromise. To keep the weight down I decided on just one DSLR body – a Canon 450D – and one zoom lens, the Canon 18-55, with a Sigma DP1 compact as a backup. With these cameras I could take photos that would reproduce well at large sizes. I also carried a tripod for low light photos and self-portraits. The total weight of my camera gear was 4.8lbs/2.2kg when I set out. As it was, the compact camera lasted less than 2 weeks and so was sent home early in the walk. The DSLR made it to the end, though the autofocus failed on the lens so for the last few weeks I had to use manual focus. The smartphone also had a camera which I used very occasionally (it used up batteries fast) and photos from which appeared in the reports I sent back to TGO magazine. Printed small they looked okay. In total, with all three cameras, I took 1868 pictures.

The last camp at Cedar Creek on the Pacific coast, Olympic National Park

BIBLIOGRAPHY

Abbey, Edward *The Monkey Wrench Gang*, Penguin Modern Classics, 2004

Abbey, Edward *Abbey's Road*, Dutton, 1979

Abbey, Edward *Black Sun*, Capra, 1990

Alden, Peter and Paulson, Dennis (eds) *National Audubon Society Field Guide to the Pacific Northwest*, Knopf, 2008.

Bass, Rick *The Book of Yaak*, Houghton Mifflin, 1996

Bass, Rick, *Winter [Notes from Montana]*, Houghton Mifflin, 1991

Brown, Hamish, *Hamish's Mountain Walk*, Sandstone, 2010

Kavanagh, James and Leung, Raymond, *Montana Birds: An Introduction to Familiar Species*, Waterford Press, 2000

Kerouac, Jack *The Dharma Bums*, Penguin Modern Classics, 2007

Kerouac, Jack *Desolation Angels*, Flamingo, 2001

Lindsay, Ann and House, Syd *The Tree Collector: The Life and Explorations of David Douglas*, Aurum Press, 2005

Nisbet, Jack *The Collector: David Douglas and the Natural History of the Northwest*, Sasquatch Books, 2009

Nisbet, Jack *Sources of the River: Tracking David Thompson Across Western North America*, Sasquatch Books, 2007

Peacock, Doug *Grizzly Years: In Search of the American Wilderness* Henry Holt, 1990

Peacock, Doug and Peacock, Andrea *In the Presence of Grizzlies: the Ancient Bond Between Men and Bears* The Lyons Press, 2009

Romano, Craig *Columbia Highlands: Exploring Washington's Last Frontier* Nairi, 2007

Simmerman, Melanie *Pacific Northwest Trail Town Guide*, 2012

Snyder, Gary *A Range of Poems*, Fulcrum, 1967

Snyder, Gary *Riprap and Cold Mountain Poems*, Counterpoint, 2010

Strickland, Ron *The Pacific Northwest Trail Guide*, Sasquatch Books, 2001

Strickland, Ron *Pathfinder: Blazing a New Wilderness Trail in Modern America*, Oregon State University Press, 2011

Turner, Jack *The Abstract Wild*, University of Arizona Press, 1996

Watts, Tom, *Pacific Coast Tree Finder*, Wilderness Press, 2004

Watts, Tom and Watts, Bridget *Rocky Mountain Tree Finder*, Nature Study Guild, 2008

Web Sites

Conservation Northwest www.conservationnw.org/

Geology of Olympic National Park geomaps.wr.usgs.gov/parks/olym/index.html

Glacier National Park www.nps.gov/glac/index.htm

North Cascades National Park www.nps.gov/noca/index.htm

Olympic National Park www.nps.gov/olym/index.htm

Pacific Northwest Trail Association www.pnta.org

Ron Strickland www.ronstrickland.com

US Forest Service www.fs.fed.us/

Wilderness Areas www.wilderness.net

Page following: A huge view from the summit of Abercrombie Mountain, Selkirk Mountains